# Ordinary Mysteries

*More Chronicles of Life, Love and Laughter*

# Ordinary Mysteries

*More Chronicles of Life, Love and Laughter*

By
Stephen J. Vicchio

*Wakefield Editions*
A Subsidiary of Christian Classics, Inc.
Post Office Box 30
Westminster, Maryland 21157
1991

FIRST PUBLISHED 1991
© 1991 BY STEPHEN J. VICCHIO

ISBN: 087061 184 4
LIBRARY OF CONGRESS CARD CATALOG NUMBER: 91-65687

COMPOSITION BY: WORDWIFERY
RR01 BOX 123A, WILLIAMSBURG, MA 01096

PRINTED IN THE USA

*For Kathleen and Owen—
like the sun, constant sources of warmth and light.*

*Mysteries are not necessarily miracles.*

—GOETHE

# *Table of Contents*

Preface ................................................................. xiii

*Ordinary Mysteries:* An Introduction .......................... xvii

## Childhood
Summer Camp ..........................................................3
Time Present ............................................................6
In Search of Lincoln Logs ...........................................9
Gladys' Ghostly Tragedy ..........................................12
The Incinerator .......................................................15
The Faith of Children ...............................................19
A Hair Piece ...........................................................21
Cold War Christmas ................................................23

## Nature
Free Rain ...............................................................27
Sounds of Cicada ....................................................29
Borrowers of Light ..................................................32
A Dog in the Moonlight ............................................35
As the Crickets' Chorus Fades ...................................37
Snow and the Best of Baltimore .................................39
He Who Plants Trees ................................................41
Music is its Roar .....................................................44

## Politics
Why Did We Drop the Second Bomb? ........................49
Done in the Style of the Double-T .............................54
Say It Again, Dan ...................................................57
Goals ....................................................................59
How to Solve the Congressional Pay Dilemma ............62
Supreme Court Joins the Blood-Revenge Crowd .........64

A Proper Guest List ........................................................67
Dogs without Heroes ......................................................70
The Tragedy of Marion Barry .......................................72

## *Good and Evil*
Indissoluble Ties ............................................................77
The Meese Pornography Commission ........................79
Knowing a Good Man When We See One ...................84
Meditations on the Nuclear Age ...................................87
See No Evil .....................................................................90
Klaus Barbie ...................................................................93
Thoughts on the Death of Bruno Bettleheim ................96
Furnace for Your Foe .....................................................99

## *Religion*
Religion in the '80s ......................................................105
The Vatican and Contraception ...................................111
Religion and Hats .........................................................114
How To Play Both Sides of Creation Street ...............117
Know Them by Their Fingernails ...............................121
Giving Christ a Bad Name ...........................................124
An Irony at the Vatican ................................................126
The Infinite Became Finite in a Tiny Child ...............129

## *Reading, Writing and Teaching*
Dancing with My Students ..........................................133
Writing about Writing ..................................................136
Mencken, A Life ...........................................................140
The Whole Megilla .......................................................142
Dropping a Rose Petal ..................................................144
Blessed Rage for Order Forms ....................................147
The Eclectic Chair ........................................................149
Reunion and the Problem of Change ..........................151
On Hand Raising ..........................................................154
On Visiting Poe with Borges .......................................157
Finding the Words ........................................................161

## *Travel*
From Baltimore to Baltimore .................................167

## *Love*
On Not Writing about My Mother ..............................193
Talking to Myself ..........................................195
The Uses of Tears ..........................................197
Death of a Drugstore .......................................200
The Cloud Velocity Detection Position ......................203
Sappho and the Bittersweet .................................206
Dancing with My Sisters ....................................209
The Old Neighborhood .......................................212

## *Scattered Pieces*
Baseball: Spring's First Great Conviction ..................217
Talking to Dogs ............................................220
Pictures from the Radio ....................................222
Odd Glitches ...............................................227
K-Mart and Neurosurgery ....................................229
The Department of Lost Things ..............................231
Stretch Limousines .........................................233
The Return of Mundane Mysteries ............................235
The Real Mr. Potato Head ...................................238
Alphabetical Discrimination ................................241
On Seeing Time .............................................243

# *Preface*

For journalists—semi-literate, most of us—a book that opens friendly doors into the ramparts of the philosophers is balm for our sense of intellectual inferiority. Stephen Vicchio opens those doors, and more effectively than your average philosopher because his scholarly insights deal mainly with the mundane matters of journalism. Not many of us can buttress our news stories with just the right phrase from James Joyce, Dante, and Dostoevsky—all in the same short story.

But I introduce this book as if it were ponderous. To the contrary, reading many of these essays is something close to *fun.* I use that word with some hesitation. A number of Vicchio's pieces are, indeed, delightfully *funny,* but more of them enlighten and challenge and provoke, all of which set the neural juices flowing and instill a sense of excitement. That, to an active mind, is sheer pleasure. To be sure, if he deals with reminiscences about his childhood toys, he also wrestles with the moral agony involved in the dropping of the first atomic bomb, or the trial of Klaus Barbie. He is, in point of fact, a scholar whose doctoral thesis confronts the question of how evil can exist in a world watched over by an all-good and omnipotent God.

Is Vicchio a philosopher or a teacher of philosophy? I don't know which he would prefer, but as the editor who was among the first to publish his essays, I would beg the question and say Stephen Vicchio is a writer. Consider his elegy for the now-decaying community where he grew up: "It is a neighborhood dying, dying of a thousand disappointments." He regrets that in his childhood toy, "Mr. Potato Head," the real potato has been replaced with a plastic imitation, terminating the era when "a child could place the eyes, ears, nose, and mouth anywhere he or she liked, often creating potatoes like Salvador Dali might have made if he were God." In discussing Michel de Montaigne, the father of essayists, Vicchio observes that "multiple personalities lounged around in the vacant space of a single head, like cab drivers sitting around the garage waiting for the next fare from the dispatcher. There was no telling who would get the next ride." That simile, not surprisingly, might also have been applied to essayist Vicchio.

Vicchio probes the dark and distressing corners of the human mind with an underlying reverence for life. The evils of the death penalty (imposed far more often on blacks than whites under identical circumstances) disturb him profoundly: "blood revenge under the grim guise of justice." His assessment of Col. Oliver North, convicted of charges related to the Iran-Contra scandal, is that here "is clearly a courageous man," but "courageous men are not always good men."

On public moral issues, there is also the practical Vicchio. What should be the answer to the infusion of pornography in our society? The seeming collective outrage over pornography is belied by the relentless demand for it. For a perceptive and simple solution, I recommend his essay on the Meese Pornography Commission. Perhaps only a philosopher could be so practical.

Like Montaigne, Vicchio speaks in many voices. There is something here for everyone: childhood, politics, nature, religion, and baseball (a subcategory of religion?). Travel, too: imagine a round-trip from Baltimore to Tulsa on a succession of Greyhound buses just for the pleasure of observing the behavior of the human species.

The author is no cloistered monk. He plays basketball, reads the newspaper assiduously, and is ceaselessly interested in everything from science to chamber music to the comic strips.

On baseball, I grab an ex-editor's rare opportunity to one-up a learned philosopher. One of my favorites of his essays deals with baseball's adherence not to the ancient

Greek concept of *kronos* (clock time) that externally constricts football and basketball, but internally by *kairos,* another Greek work that connotes the "right" time. In modern Greek, which I know slightly, the word *kairos* survives. It connotes not only "time," in the sense of weather (as *temps* in French), but is used specifically in *kalokairi,* which literally means "good weather" but also "summertime." *Kalokairi* seems to be a word made for the summer game.

Vicchio's gems include an essay on essays, with frequent reference to Montaigne: writes Vicchio "The essayist...is already congenitally predisposed to believing that all he thinks about is interesting—that others are amused by conversations he has with himself."

In the case of the pages that follow, we can be grateful that Stephen Vicchio was so congenitally predisposed.

Gwinn Owens<br>
Retired Editor<br>
*Baltimore Evening Sun*

# *Ordinary Mysteries: An Introduction*

Experience and desire are so often conspirators. They conspire to make of a life an ordinary thing—and they usually succeed. Our ordinary minds—the ones that arrive at work by nine on Monday—usually demand an ordinary world, one that can be inhabited more comfortably. Indeed, ordinary minds seem to feel most at ease when they have taken for granted even the ordinary world.

In looking back at these pieces, mostly written over the past four years, one thread that seems to run through them is that I most often write about the ordinary. These essays (a word that two editors have now counselled me against using) are about street signs, toy stores, and what the beach is like just before nightfall. In these pages I give an account of my neighborhood drugstore, the Russian wolfhound who shared my house for ten years, and what it is like to teach philosophy in a small college that continues to hold the liberal arts tradition in its firm grasp.

If I have a persona that dominates these essays, it is frequently that of a bemused fly on the wall or a magnifying glass with a mind of its own. If I can land unobtrusively on just the right wall, or apply the lens at just the proper angle, the ordinary, at least to me, becomes mysterious.

This collection contains other pieces where I attempt to make some small bit of sense of events and people who in no way could be seen as ordinary: the bloodshed in China in the Summer of 1989; the Iran-Contra trial of Oliver North; and the conviction of Klaus Barbie for atrocities committed as one frame in a macabre collection of willful acts to which we now refer by using a term formerly reserved for a kind of natural disaster: Holocaust.

It is difficult for the writer to keep himself out of these pieces, and so I make no real attempt to separate myself from the events or the personalities who shaped them. About Klaus Barbie one ought not to assume the role of bemused fly on the wall.

Several of these essays have appeared elsewhere, about half of them in the *Baltimore Evening Sun,* the *Baltimore Sun, Cadenza* and *The Maryland Poetry Review.* Others originally came to life as commentaries for WJHU, the Johns Hopkins University's public radio station in Baltimore.

I might thank any number of people for their help in the publication of this book. I will surely leave out many who deserve mention. John McHale, the publisher, ought to be thanked for taking a chance on yet another book. Gwinn Owens, my former editor and continual friend, provided a thoughtful preface. Julia Thorpe, Peg Cermak, Maureen Robinson and Christine Creager helped in the preparation of the manuscript. Elizabeth McHale served admirably in the dual role of editor and typesetter. Cathie Brettschneider read the manuscript with the care of a friend and the eye of an editor. My wife, Kathleen Cahill, and our son, Owen, continually make writing and living as valuable as I can imagine it being. It is to them this book is dedicated.

Collections of essays are most like a family reunion. It is, at least for many of us, a rare, almost artificial occasion where odd and disparate individuals get together to celebrate their shared accident of birth. At most family reunions you might hear the same tales more than once. That may happen in these pages as well. But you might give these essays at least a bit of indulgence. They have been brought together only quite recently. Before then, they had been happily leading their individual lives in the pages of now-yellowed newspapers, in the bottom drawer of my oak desk, or in radio waves that my scientist friends tell me are still traveling in space.

Baltimore, Fall, 1990                                        S.J.V.

# Childhood

*Childhood shows the man,
as morning shows the day.*
—JOHN MILTON

# Summer Camp

My parents sent me to camp when I was six. My mother was not so sure about it: three weeks away from home. That first year I endured it. When they visited on parents' day, I pretended to love it. I knew, even then, it was the struggle for independence that kept me from telling them about my longing for home.

In the second summer, and for many summers after that, I stayed the full six weeks and loved it. My time was spent swimming, boating, and telling small lies about home.

It is difficult to write about camp without profoundly altering the experiences. In plucking the fruit of memory one always runs the risk of spoiling the bloom. Much of my camp experiences lie hidden away in that region of half-memory. It is a province where things lie forgotten unless they clamor for help in dreams.

In all that raw material of summer experience my memory seems always to run back to three incidents. What they have in common is a movement away from an idyllic picture of the world. They are stories about a loss of innocence. They are tales about wanting to be older and wiser than I really was.

In my second year at camp I was assigned a lower bunk, a special kind of ignominy for a seven year old. If one could add injury to insult, it happened when a boy named Peter Pierce was given the top bunk. By the end of the first week Peter had acquired the nickname "Pee-pot." The origin of the name should be obvious. Pee-pot had developed his own version of the trickle down theory. In the morning the counsellors hauled out Pee-pot's mattress and mine. They aired them out side by side, on the hill next to the bunk house. Two hundred campers saw them on their return from breakfast.

The older boys thought I shared Pee-pot's problem. I tried hard to dissociate myself by jeering at him in an especially derisive way. I had my bunk changed to the other side of the room. I would not let the boy pass without offering some wounding comment about his lack of control.

The summers that followed were full of capture the flag, relay races, and softball, but Peter Pierce never returned.

A few summers later, two older boys had managed to drill a small peep-hole in the wall we shared with the ladies' dressing room. Sunday was family day. While others were swimming, we three began a catalog of what our fellow campers' mothers and sisters looked like without their clothes on.

I knew at the time I did not understand. I pretended to be like the older boys until one afternoon they told me what my sisters looked like without their bathing tops. There is a sweet almost indefinable irony about innocence. I think I first learned it that day. There is little hope for innocence unless it is recognized. And yet, one only becomes aware of it after it is irretrievably lost.

By my fifth summer at camp, innocence had mingled with experience, like red swimming ribbons in too many summers of lake water. By then, I had learned the secret steps to receiving one of the ten coveted "best camper" awards. One needed to run fast, swim far, and never lose a piece of underwear.

Like the four summers before, my mother had dutifully sewn into all my belongings little name tags declaring me the undisputed owner of these articles. On the first day of my fifth year at camp I borrowed scissors from the Italian priest who doubled as chaplain and barber, and I clipped out the incriminating tags.

On the final day of camp—before Catholic station wagons could be seen kicking up dust on the winding road leading to the bunk house—all the campers were assembled on the hill. Several counsellors stood at the bottom with enormous cardboard boxes filled with lost underwear. Each piece was picked up and officially examined for identification.

Anything not owned up to was enthusiastically claimed by the Gallaghers, a poor family of thirteen that included seven slow-footed dog paddlers. The Gallagher boys returned home each summer with underwear for the school year. I brought home an empty suitcase and a piece of construction paper declaring me one of the ten best campers. Sometimes in the sixth grade I would look over at the next urinal to discover Michael Gallagher. I smiled a secret smile knowing he was wearing my jockey shorts. There was something about it that reminded me of what the nuns called the communion of saints.

Now, many summers later, when the temperature inches above ninety degrees, and I look out my car window at the heat shimmering just a foot or so above the sun-baked highway, I think about the Gallagher boys driving home from camp with their parents and a station wagon full of other people's underwear. And sometimes I wonder if the boys who made the tiny peep-hole in the wall of the bunk house might now have daughters of their own. And sometimes, on very warm summer nights, when it is late and even the crickets have gone to sleep, I wonder a little about Peter Pierce.

*July, 1988*

# Time Present

> *Time present and time past are*
> *both perhaps present in time future*
> *and time future contained in time past.*
> T.S. Eliot, *Four Quartets*

I stopped by my parents' house the other day. My mother had placed on one of the pieces of her living room furniture the photograph of a thin, tow-headed boy, clutching a large, tongue-stretched collie. The boy wraps his skinny arm around the dog's neck, while the other arm rests uncomfortably by his side. A half-smile is spread for the camera.

Although it is a photo of me, I speak of the boy as if he were another. In her novel *Jacob's Room,* Virginia Woolf talks about each of us having a self shut up inside like the leaves of a book known only to the author by heart. All others may glimpse only at the title page unless read to by the one who lives within.

There is something troubling and yet fascinating about looking at the photograph. I am simultaneously the reader and the one read to. I search the picture looking for something, clues perhaps, but clues to what? Each of us is a history-making creature. We construct ourselves out of wants and fears. We cannot repeat the past, nor can we fully leave it behind. There are ghosts in all of our lives, but some of the most haunting ones are the children we once were. The past cannot bury itself. It perches just on the edge of the present waiting somehow to be admitted to the present. But I cannot quite do it when looking at the photograph.

Over a trackless past lies, somehow, the boy I once was. He stares at me from the picture. How have I become the man I am? Where did the little boy go? And why do I feel such an overwhelming sadness when looking at the photograph?

It is true that one cannot be the judge of another's grief. But with this boy in the photograph, my judgment of grief must be quite different. I am both the dead and the bereaved. When I stare at his eyes, I know what they will see, from the inside, for the next thirty-five years. I know the mistakes they will make, the things they will not see, the sorrows. I want to say to this child, the ghost trapped with a dog dead thirty years, *be careful, be careful.*

I search the photo for the scar at the edge of my hair line, the result of an encounter of a runaway tricycle with a common household broomstick. The scar was not there. It would come in a few years. There is no split in my upper lip, and no mark beneath my left eye. These, and most of the scars that cannot so readily be seen, all await the boy in the photograph.

A moment later, while standing alone in the living room, there rose up in me a feeling that I, along with thoughtless others, will have caused these scars. The feeling was clear and distinct. It is like visiting the grave of a friend I have injured. Death has prevented me from making the necessary reparation. And it is this, I think, that is the real source of sorrow. Only age and sorrow have that particular gift of reading the future by a sad past.

As I stared at the picture, I wanted to hold the hand of the boy, I wanted to perform some strange act of magic in which my grasping the slender fingers of that unhappy child, I could heal the past.

The following morning, on the long drive to my office, I could not lose this image of holding the boy's hand. This caused me somehow to think about the man whom I wish to become someday: older, and certainly wiser—and full of a kind of courage I do not now possess. And in the midst of this thinking there arose a fuller image, a picture from a special region of the imagination. In this larger picture one of my hands reaches for the little boy until our fingers meet. My other hand stretches out into the future, until it finds the fingers of that man I hope someday to be. For the briefest of moments we connect. And in that instant that was a lifetime the world is knitted together with my two hands.

Someday, perhaps in another thirty-five years, I will look back at that moment. I will need the younger man now tied to the child. The pictures from that special province of the imagination will be about the past. Memory will do the work of my two hands. Memory, in an instant, will try somehow to knit together what was a lifetime.

*September, 1988*

# In Search of Lincoln Logs

Last week I went in search of Lincoln Logs. A friend's son was having a birthday, and I thought the little brown logs with the green slats for the roof would make a great present.

I went to a toy store that looks like an airplane hangar. You know the one: outside there is a giraffe holding a sign written by someone suffering from dyslexia, faulty syntax, and a penchant for spelling simple words phonetically.

At first, the Lincoln Logs were nowhere to be found. Nor was the feeling that I was in a toy store. The atmosphere was more like a gigantic supermarket where one might expect to find patrons pulling Barbie and Ken from the shelves so they might be sauteed for dinner.

When I was a small child most of my important toys were made of wood. One could imagine they were crafted by a little old man sitting in a workshop in Vienna. Tufts of white hair protruded from the sides of his shiny bald head, his sparkling blue eyes peered intently through square-framed glasses which pinched the end of his nose. The old craftsman sat patiently painting the toys with delicate brush.

Most small toys these days are made of dichlorobicycletricyclepolyacetatebutylmethyltriplasticate. The ingredients for these toys conjure up images of men wearing white lab coats, protective goggles, and yellow rubber gloves. One can imagine neatly-lettered signs in the lab warning these men to wear their protective equipment at all times.

The toy soldiers in my childhood stood about three to five inches high. They were often made of lead. The chemical symbol for lead is Pb. The toy soldiers of today are one or two inches tall. They are made of dichlorobicycletricyclepolyacetatebutylmethyltriplasticate. There seems to be a curious phenomenon at work here. As the toy soldiers have become progressively smaller, the chemical structure for their composition has become progressively larger. At this rate, my grandchildren will be playing with their toy soldiers under a microscope, but the manufacturers won't be able to fit the table of contents on the box.

The most disquieting discovery I have made in my search for Lincoln Logs is that most of my favorite toys are gone forever, or in some cases radically changed. Mexican jumping beans and the little acrobat who does a flip when you press two sticks joined by a string were nowhere to be found. I didn't see the kind of roller skates where you use a key and have to wear what my mother called "good shoes." I searched in vain for a magic slate, the mysterious shiny grey paper that stuck to the black wax background. When you wanted to erase what was written, you lifted the grey paper that made a noise like cheap trousers ripping. I found some slinkies. But they are now made of dichlorobicycletricyclepolyacetatebutylmethyltriplasticate, so they no longer make the little slinking noise when they walk down the stairs.

Other toys I hated as a child—like the demented chimpanzee with the red fez who beats on the xylophone—were still there. After twenty-five years of practice, the monkey's music still has not progressed beyond a random expression of simple notes.

After about an hour of searching, I finally found the Lincoln Logs. They had been there all along, but they were so small I didn't recognize them. A Lincoln Log has always been roughly the size of a tootsie roll. If you have seen a tootsie roll lately, you know what has happened to the Lincoln Logs. It doesn't seem right to call them Lincoln Logs anymore. You could never get a lead president with a stove pipe hat into a cabin made of those things. You could hardly fit in a couple of toy soldiers made of dichlorobicycletricyclepolyacetatebutylmethyltriplasticate.

*June, 1987*

# Ghostly Tragedy

Gladys Finkenbinder. The very name hints at comedy, a wry smile seems involuntarily to smooth the creases of one's lips. But Gladys Finkenbinder's story was no comedy. There was a kind of inevitability to her tale. It was almost a Greek tragedy, except for the fact that Aristotle says the tragic hero somehow starts out nobler than the rest of us. Gladys was made of the same stuff as all of us, a few parts protoplasm, a few parts imagination. The other morning she died in a fire in her Irvington home where she lived as a prisoner, a captive to the ghosts who haunted the middle of her head.

Firefighters found her in a four-foot pile of newspapers and trash in the kitchen. The candles she used for light and heat, and to keep away those ghosts, ignited the papers and killed her.

And so Gladys was a tragic hero. But she was no Oedipus, though surely she was just as blind. She was no Antigone. But she had that same intractable will, the fierce kind of independence that sometimes must act against its own self-interest. She suffered from the same kind of metaphysical homelessness as the best of Athenian and Elizabethan heroes, for like them, the ghosts had evicted her from her own head. Gladys Finkenbinder was as confused as Othello and Hamlet, and King Lear, that madman mumbling to himself on the heath. And now her confusion has killed her.

For those of us who lived nearby, for those of us who might have helped had the ghosts given their permission, the inevitability seems so much clearer now. And that is the way tragedy always goes: we only have the full picture after the fate of the tragic figure is sealed. It is at the very moment the tragedy becomes clear that we realize we can do nothing about it.

Gladys lived in a place where the ghosts were always throwing their voices. What was inside her skull always sounded like it was coming from outside the house. She had more difficulty than the rest of us in giving a proper name to the terrible. And then it killed her. The problem was one of geography. Just like Othello and Oedipus, Gladys thought the problem was outside. It turned out to be inside. She didn't live long enough to find out.

In the evening newspaper, in a story placed next to the tale of a living two-day-old child left in a trash bag amid the debris of a yard in the 2200 block of Greenmount Avenue, Gladys Finkenbinder's story of inevitability could be found. The chronicler of Gladys' tale said that the heavy plastic she had taped to her windows kept the cold out, but also prevented quick detection of the fire. The writer of Gladys' story could not have known the real reason for the plastic. It was to keep the voices out. But Gladys had no way of knowing where the voices really lived. There was no plastic she could erect to ward off the ghosts in her head.

In the end of Gladys' story the writer gave some important hints about heating methods we should avoid in winter: don't heat the house by turning on a gas oven or burner; don't heat your home with portable kerosene heaters; don't heat your home with candles.

The writer who wrote the end of Gladys' story could not have known about the inevitability that contained the old woman's death, that the death was wrapped up in her head along with the ghosts. The writer could not have known the words she wrote about Gladys, well-meaning words of instruction and warning, had nothing to do with Gladys Finkenbinder. The writer of the end of the tale could not have known that her words were like witnessing the fated carnage of the final scene of *Hamlet* and then commenting that one should be careful when handling sharp objects.

*December, 1988*

# The Incinerator

There is a particular kind of dark red brick that is inextricably connected, by force of memory, to my early school years. Proust reminds us that memory is usually hidden somewhere outside the realm of intellect—that it sometimes resides instead in material objects, objects that will give us, sometimes when we do not suspect it, a pristine picture of the past; such is the case with dark, fire-burnt red brick.

In my Catholic childhood, there were the old school and the new school, both constructed of that same red brick. The only difference between the two was the toll weather and the passage of time had taken on the two buildings. The old school was a darker shade, the color children's tongues turn when they have eaten black licorice. The brick of the new school was fresher, cleaner, with faint veins of blue running through it, like the underside of those same tongues.

The two schools were connected by a long, dark hallway. Old brick met new at the principal's office. Only a mind for detail would detect the subtle change in the brickwork outside. If one spent much time, as I did, in the principal's office, the difference between the two shades of red brick became indelibly impressed, like initials surreptitiously carved in the wooden top of a wrought-iron desk.

The principal's office was a cramped antiseptic smelling room presided over by a cramped antiseptic principal. Imagination told me the grey navy surplus filing cabinets which lined the black linoleum floor were crammed full of report cards and permanent records of students past and present. The permanent record was a kind of parochial school rap-sheet much discussed by the principal. It catalogued offenses against school and God, both mortal and venial, real and imagined.

Outside—where the two schools met—there was a huge incinerator presided over by Mr. O'Brien, a gaunt and taciturn old man who divided his time between the incinerator and spreading sawdust on second- and third-grade stomach troubles left in the old school's hallways.

One could get a glimpse of the inner working of the incinerator if lucky enough to be picked by one of the nuns to carry the ribbed metal, olive-drab trash cans full of balled-up loose-leaf paper, pencil shavings, and pint-sized chocolate milk containers from the Wilton Farm Dairy. The wax on the milk cartons would sizzle for the briefest of moments before being consumed by flame.

When Mr. O'Brien opened the huge iron door, the hot blast of air was like walking out of the air-conditioned Irvington Theatre into a sweltering August day. There was the searing heat and glare that made one see red rings of fire even with one's eyes closed.

But the theatre and the school, though two blocks apart, existed in different worlds. The incinerator reminded me of stories about hell, and Mr. O'Brien was the keeper of the gates. The movie house was a way of escaping those stories. There was nothing at all menacing about the usher at the Irvington Theatre. He was a myopic, bent-over old man full of sorrow and a deep tubercular cough. He regularly ordered us to remove our feet from the seats in front. He could never find the right boys who made that funny party-favor honking noise by blowing into an empty Juicy Fruit box.

In the dark of the theatre it was easy to escape retributive justice. There was nothing about the movie house that hinted at eternal damnation.

The open incinerator was different; the raging fire reduced anything thrown there to curled black ash. School for me in those years was dominated by the image of that incinerator and the eyes of Mr. O'Brien that somehow captured the light and heat of the fire there. The incinerator showed up in my dreams. I was often placed kicking and screaming into it—the punishment for failure to line up my desk on the proper linoleum squares of my third-grade classroom. I seemed always to be one linoleum square out of line. In my dreaming state, I believed one only received so many chances, and then matters were left in the hands of the stubble-faced Mr. O'Brien and those fiery eyes. James Joyce in a *Portrait of the Artist* talks about Stephen's brain simmering and bubbling within the cracking tenement of his skull. Flames burst forth from his cranium "like a corolla, shrieking like voices." Daedelus might have carried a bent metal trash can to his grade school incinerator.

I have come to see in recently years that it was not the incinerator but the classroom that more resembled Dante's "sorrowful city." I don't dream much these days about Mr. O'Brien and the incinerator. But late at night when I take dream air into my lungs, and slip below the level of consciousness, down, down to those deep pools of remembrance, I often find my grade school classroom. There I find a suffering that comes with the consciousness that one is not quite loved enough. Aloysha Karamazov believed that this is the definition of hell. In those red brick buildings with a crucifix in every room affixed to the wall above the loudspeaker, we did all the difficult things: we read, we wrote, we spelled, we fasted, we prayed, but we were not taught enough to do the simple one—we did not learn to love enough.

Like Dante's hell, there was no hope there, nothing to be gained by prayer. Salvation came by works, not through grace.

In recent years I have wondered just how much my grade school experiences have determined the man I have become. I am afraid I still worry a little too much about my permanent record. I am fearful about the difficulty, or perhaps the impossibility, of a love full of grace.

I want to return, as I did last night in a dream, to dismantle the incinerator. I want to fire Mr. O'Brien. I want to find that third-grade classroom with students freeze-dried in some strange suspended animation of 1959. I want to find myself in the second row, the next to the last seat, a skinny boy with a crooked smile. I want to whisper into the ear of that confused but well-meaning nun: *Teach that little boy in the second row how to love.*

And then, I want her to make an announcement that class is dismissed because we are all going to the movies at the Irvington Theatre.

*August, 1988*

# The Faith of Children

The other evening while doing a magic trick for the children of some friends, I was discovered. The cleverly palmed dime was not so cleverly palmed. The six-year-old, the younger of the two boys, made his disappointment known. His brother, a more worldly eleven-year-old, gave me a secret wink.

Of course it is usually the Chanukah/Christmas season that is associated with the childlike anticipation of the six-year-old, and the inevitable disappointment. But I found later on that in this week of Passover and Easter the smaller boy was willing to give the mysterious, the magical, another chance.

Later in the evening, while he was sitting on the hooked rug by the fire, I began secretly to toss coins in the air so that they might land near the boy. In a short while he was convinced they had magically fallen from the ceiling.

In adulthood each of us begins to believe there is a great distance between us and the children we once were. It is not just the gullibility of the child we wish to deny, it is also the vulnerability. And yet, in our hearts, that place that has remained the same size since childhood, we know the gulf separating us from our earliest years is really not so great. Memory reminds us of the infinite vastness to which we all, as children, awakened in the middle of the night. The darkness of childhood was populated by an array of creatures too frightening even to have names.

Faith, in those early years, was often a tiny night light kept burning by the bed of the small child. As long as the child knew it was there, the obscurity could not be complete. The child awakened from the worst of dreams to search for the light, mostly because it reminded him that the daylight would soon come.

In adulthood faith often seems so much more difficult, but it is something one never really loses. For even the most skeptical of us, faith is a great vessel into which we all must pour the liquid of the self. What one chooses to believe without sufficient evidence may be very different from the next person, but that we must believe, I think, is undeniable.

For Jews, Passover is a time that requires the faith of a child. Perhaps this is why in the traditional Seder service it is the youngest child who is asked why this night is different from any other. Passover celebrates that, despite what history and experience tell us, the Israelites have been a chosen people.

Leo Baeck speaks of the essence of Judaism as "the capacity to perceive the abiding in the transitory, the invisible in the visible." In the twentieth century, a time that has seen those monsters of childhood come to life, it takes nothing less than the faith of a child to believe that Baeck is right.

Christians in the Easter season must also take on the hope of a child when asking whether it is more difficult to be born or to rise again. Pascal puts the mystery this way in his *Pensees:*

> Is it more amazing that what has never been should be, or that what has been should be again? Is it more difficult to come into being than to return to it?

If both Passover and Easter tell us anything today, it is that faith, like the hopes of children, is durable and miraculous. You may put it in the grave, but it won't stay there. You can send it to a death camp or nail it to a cross, you can lock it up in a gas chamber or wrap it in a winding sheet and shut it in a tomb, but it will always, always rise again.

*April, 1990*

# A Hairpiece

When I was a boy I had my hair cut at Harry's Barbershop. In the window was a small statue of Popeye. The gold painted sailor stood there, forearms bulging, corncob pipe in hand. What I liked most about the statue was its location. The chipped plaster-of-Paris Popeye, frozen in a characteristic action pose, had only a few discernible hairs on his head. From that barbershop window he winked at the world, as if the entire idea struck him as funny enough to be passed over in silence.

Inside the shop, the chairs were manned by the establishment's namesake, a tall thin man with a great memory and a gift for the understatement. His partner, a man called Buddy, took part in the paradox. He wore a red toupee and a look of permanent disagreeableness. When Buddy spoke, it was mostly about Blacks. A special scorn seemed to be reserved only for them. The rest of us received Buddy's regular variety of unpleasantness. I used to sit waiting for my turn, hoping I would land in Harry's chair.

I write about all this now because we no longer refer to the places we have our hair done as barbershops and beauty parlors. *Beauty parlor.* It sounded so mysterious and ethereal—the kind of place where amazing transformation might have taken place.

These days the word "hair" is no longer used principally as a noun. It has taken on the job of an adjective, mostly in connection with the names of places of business. I began musing about this the other day when a friend told me she has her hair done at a place called the Hair Explosion. I wonder what kind of fallout is produced in a hair explosion. The Hair Affair, the Hair Conspiracy, the Hair Garage and the Hair Extraordinaire have replaced beauty parlors and barbershops.

Today people are lined up to get their hair cut at places with names like the Hair Harbor, the Hair Harvest or the Hair Loft. If you are aeronautically oriented you can try the Hair Port, the Hair Force or the Hair Above.

I wonder what kind of confidence a name like Hair Limited inspires in prospective customers. It's probably a little better than Hair Today. You know what they say: gone tomorrow.

There are Hair Pizazz, Hair Phonics, Hair Reflections, Hair Connections, the Hair Shack, the Hair Shop and I wish I weren't making up some of this.

You might decide to entrust your locks to the Hair Dynasty, Hair in Motion or the Hair Pair. For those of you struggling with a problem of personal identity, you might try the Hair We Are. There are the Hair Anatomy, the Hair Dimensions, and for those who think globally, Hair World.

I don't think I want to have my hair cut at any of these places. Unless, of course, they put a statue of Popeye in the window.

I'm sure he'd still be winking.

*May, 1988*

# Cold War Christmas

I came into the world around Christmastime. It was just a few years after the birth of the Cold War. I considered the Cold War a sibling of sorts, a kind of adoptive brother who had taken up residence at my house before my arrival that holiday season.

A few years later, Senator Joseph McCarthy was finding communists seated behind too many desks in Washington. At school we were hiding beneath our seats, small fingers tightly gripped around the black wrought-iron legs of our wooden desks, six- and seven-year-olds forced to contemplate the transitory nature of things. The process was called "ducking and covering" in the Civil Defense Manual. One optimistic nun called it "atomic bomb practice." She pronounced the words as if she were saying "Christmas play practice," wanting us to get it right in dress rehearsal so we'd do well in the real performance.

Around the time of the Cuban missile crisis, the sisters made atomic bomb practice a regular part of our school week. While hiding beneath my desk, it occurred to me that, thanks to the teacher's meticulously kept seating chart, if the bomb were to drop, my classmates and I would all die in alphabetical order.

Cold War Christmas was always a strange combination of celebration and foreboding. We sang songs about the Prince of Peace and hid Christmas presents in bomb shelters waiting for the big day to come. One of my cub scout projects was completed just a few days before our holiday vacation. It consisted of the building of an intercontinental missile fashioned from orange juice cans and a toilet paper husk retrieved from the bathroom trash.

I began thinking about Cold War Christmases this morning when I went exploring in the woods with a friend's three-year-old son. We moved down a narrow path to a clearing where snow lay untouched but for one set of clear tracks made by a white tail fox who is a frequent visitor to the edge of the boy's family property.

The snow was a fine powder—the kind that makes no sound when disturbed by footprints. As children we called it "silent snow," an expression that survivors of Hiroshima used to describe the radioactive soot that rained on their city for days after the explosion in 1945.

This morning while cutting holly with the boy I stared at a sky the color of blue irises. It lay crisp and clear just above the tree line. For a moment I thought of all those Cold War Christmases. In those years we understood the idea of peace as nothing more than the absence of war. Perhaps this is because in our time, since that day in August of 1945 when Pandora opened the lid and invited us to rummage through her box, we have comprehended that the real opposite of that kind of peace is not war. It is annihilation.

John Milton suggests that peace, no less than war, sometimes has its victories. With the changes sweeping across eastern Europe this holiday season, this may be the first Christmas in my lifetime where the expression "peace on earth" may really mean something. I thought about that as the boy and I moved back toward the path leading out of the woods. We carried holly and the few sticks small boys always collect on such occasions.

As we arrived at the gate, he began to sing softly as he waved one of the sticks like a conductor's baton. I unfastened the latch, swung open the gate, and bent down so I could hear the song. The boy's cheeks were that pink color one gets with a morning of clipping holly in the woods. He was just finishing the refrain, which was accompanied by a sweeping motion of the baton: "It's a small, small world."

*December, 1989*

# Nature

*Surely there is something in the unruffled calm
of nature that overawes our little anxieties and
doubts: the sight of the deep blue sky, the clustering
stars above, seem to impart a quiet to the mind.*
—Jonathan Edwards

# Free Rain

I have been meaning for some time to write about the rain. It just occurred to me I should do it now while it's still free of charge, while it still happens when and where it wishes. The time will come, I fear, when the rain will be bought and sold. We are already selling the air. I bought some yesterday at a gas station. I dropped my quarter into something called an "aeromatic." A compressor coughed into service and I was allotted my fair share.

It can't be long before someone will go into the business of rain. Some clever person will make a corporation, and the corporation will make rain. Later, someone will develop new and improved rain. By then, all the gratuity and unpurposefulness of rain will be gone. Rain futures will be bought and sold. We will no longer pray for rain. Stockbrokers will.

But this evening the rain is still free. It is coming down in buckets and torrents, in cats and dogs. It is raining to beat the band. It dashes in enormous drops against the window. The drops narrow to rivers, then silently slide down the pane until puddles form on the sill, like tiny individual souls merging with Brahma in Hindu mythology.

For years I have wondered why in the city we run to escape the rain. People with folded newspapers over their heads scatter along the sidewalk, like ants agitated by some gigantic stick. For us, rain no longer means renewal. We do not see that the streets shine beautifully in the rain, and that in summer rain, mysterious steam rises from the cooling asphalt, if only we will look.

For those of us in the city, the rain is an inconvenience. It is something we don't yet control. But after the business sector has had a crack at it, the rain problem will be solved. The solution will put people back to work. It will help the economy. We will compete against Japanese rain.

Rain was different in the ancient world. The Hebrew prophet Elijah stood alone on Mount Carmel against 450 Baal prophets. From morning until noon the Baal holy men whirled around a sacrificial altar in a grotesque limping dance, and in a frenzy cut themselves with lances, a kind of imitative magic so that the rain might come.

The ancient Jews loved the rain. In a land where it rained very little, and only from December to February, the ancient Hebrew language still had four different words for rain.

But the ancients were so much better at admitting that life and death, and the rain were out of their control. They did not spend six minutes of their half-hour evening news trying to avoid the rain, for they knew it beat by its own secret metronome.

Elijah thought God owned the rain. And in the biblical tale, it rains only after this has been established.

We no longer believe, as the Greeks did, that rain sometimes makes mournful music or that rain is as necessary to the mind as it is to vegetation. And this is why we run from rain.

Today, when it rains in our cities, we all go a little crazy. And, at least while the storm lasts, it takes the place of our regular madness.

*August, 1987*

# Sounds of Cicada

Some say *sa-kay-ta* and some *sa-ka-ta*. Those who call them locusts are entirely wrong. Whatever one prefers to call them, the little red-eyed insects have finally arrived.

A few weeks ago I was beginning to think the coming of the cicada was like the descent of sky-lab or the appearance of Kahutek or Halley's Comet—a fairly big fuss made by the media but not much to excite the senses.

A few weeks later, I have changed my mind. Each morning there is a large collection of still-winged creatures waiting for my shoe leather to flatly confirm their demise. They lie belly-up on the sidewalk, done in by too much sex and singing. What a way to go.

For seventeen years they slept undisturbed until some strange genetic alarm clock went off in their crunchy little bodies. They hatch, climb the nearest tree, have sex, and die. It sounds more like a tryst of Tarzan and a heavy-metal rock enthusiast than a lesson in entomology.

The last time the cicada crawled above ground, I was in college and the United States was in Vietnam. In May and June of 1970, E.M. Forster, Abraham Maslow, Walter Ruether, and Gypsy Rose Lee did their dying. So did 963 American servicemen in Indochina and a handful of students at Kent State and Jackson State who made the mistake of showing up at campus demonstrations.

The last time the cicada were here Richard Nixon called campus demonstrators "bums," the trial of Charles Manson began in Los Angeles, and scientists at the University of Wisconsin announced the first complete synthesis of a single gene. Big Bird made his first appearance on *Sesame Street* in the spring of 1970, the Baltimore Orioles were on their way to a pennant and world series,

South Africa was expelled from the International Olympic Committee, and Muammar Kaddafi became the leader of Libya.

In 1953, just two cicada invasions ago, I was learning to speak in full sentences, Senator McCarthy was looking for communists, and Arthur Miller's *The Crucible* opened in New York. The first edition of *TV Guide* was published in the spring of 1953, and Burt Lancaster and Deborah Kerr were starring in *From Here to Eternity*. In early June of 1953, Watson and Crick published their first paper on the structure of the DNA molecule, and a man in the midwest invented the plastic valve for aerosol cans.

The din of the cicada reminds us how silent and gradual is the passage of time when they are not around. Ordinarily, time has no palpable divisions to mark its passing. It is invisible and inaudible, yet it inexorably moves forward. We may be able to take a step back in space, but never in time.

Because the passage of time usually goes undetected, we create artificial temporal divisions, sometimes noisy and abrupt ones like New Year's Eve, in order to call time's passage to mind. Perhaps this is the real reason we make watches that tick and clocks that chime. Without these sounds it would be too easy to believe time is an illusion.

There are apparently three different species of cicada, each making its own distinctive noise. The first makes a sound like a flying saucer or an enormous diesel engine in need of a valve job. The second sounds more like a horde of manic castanet players or hyperactive toddlers with baby rattles, each shaking to its own beat. The third kind of cicada makes the sound of an ominous cosmic busy signal.

Each of these sounds not only insures the continued survival of the species, but the pulsing, clattering and rattling make time audible. These sounds, and the sight of these strange-winged creatures, help us mark the passage of time in curious seventeen-year increments.

In a few weeks the cicada will disappear. Even after seventeen years of sleep one can only party so long before the results are disastrous. The cicada will return, if all goes well on the planet, in the year 2004. We human beings will have written another chapter about Ronald Reagan, Muammar Kaddafi, and the DNA molecule. We will have found a cure for AIDS, or it will have taken its place alongside the bubonic plague.

By 2004 many of us will have gone to our graves. Our children will be parents, or perhaps grandparents. Our first graders will be graduating from college in the spring of 2004. It will all have occurred by the awakening of one swarm of red-eyed insects.

Time will have gone sliding beneath and through our lives, beneath and through our various pains and pleasures, boredoms and elations, collective triumphs and private defeats. We will have made love, paid taxes, celebrated accomplishments and buried our dead. Time will have moved silently, invisibly, for seventeen years until the first chirping of those ugly little bugs. The cicada will once again make time visible. They will make time audible. They will make us remember in ways we usually do not.

*June, 1987*

# Borrowers of Light

*Here come real stars to fill the upper skies,
And here on earth come emulating flies.*
—Robert Frost

For those of us who live on this planet after August of 1945, it is sometimes difficult to remember that *homo sapiens* is not the inventor, nor the owner of fire. We are merely its most ardent users.

Long before Prometheus stole fire from the gods, volcanoes had belched their lower-intestinal lava into the cool air, creating smoke and heat. Lightning had struck dry grass, leaving evidence of fire in the ancient fossil record deep below the first indications of our struggle to be human.

Indeed, one of the many ways we assert that humanness is our fascination with illuminating the night. Last evening, at dusk, I watched as our four-year-old son and his seven-year-old cousin darted around the yard attempting to catch small, flying insects blessed with glowing abdomens of phosphorescent light.

The children attempted, with some success, to trap the four-winged creatures in their cupped hands. It is a tedious and delicate task. One must be swift enough to catch them, while gentle enough to keep them alive.

At the end of the evening, after all the relatives had retreated from the Father's Day celebration, the four-year-old was given a suggestion by his mother that the fireflies might be happier set free from the small mustard jar in which they had spent their benign incarceration.

The boy resisted, trying a number of excuses: that the bugs wanted to spend the night, that they were happy in the jar, that they had become his friends, that he had already given them names: *Lighteous* and *Brighteous*.

But beneath the mitigation and childish subterfuge there was something more fundamental at work in the boy. One could see it in his eyes. It was the light, and the boy's overwhelming fascination with what those tiny orange- and black-striped creatures could do with the darkness. For children, and those who are blessed with a healthy remainder of childhood, there is a point, easily reached, where the simplest facts end in mystery.

The Romans gave us the verb "to fascinate." They might have used *fascinare* to describe the fireflies' coleopterous cousins who run headlong into the bare light bulb hanging above the back porch, not in anger, but in irresistible attraction. For the Romans, *fascinare* meant to bewitch, to enchant, to come completely under a spell. That is what happened last evening in our back yard.

When we finally released the fireflies, large salty tears streamed down the boy's face. He had thought he owned the fire. He could not get used to the notion of borrowing the light.

Later in the evening, the boy had, in his own way, made a compromise with the concept of stewardship. While getting ready for bed, he asked us if we would read the poem about the fireflies, a few simple verses nearly forgotten by his parents. It was written by Paul Fleischran for two voices, and a four-year-old imagination.

| | |
|---|---|
| Light | Light |
| | is the ink we use |
| Night | Night |
| is our parchment | |
| | We're |
| | fireflies |
| fireflies | flickering |
| flitting | |

                                              flashing
fireflies
glimmering                  fireflies
                                              gleaming

glowing
Insect Calligraphers      Insect Calligraphers
practicing penmanship

                                              copying sentences
Six-legged Scribblers     Six-legged Scribblers
of vanishing messages...

*July, 1990*

# A Dog in the Moonlight

> *It is the very error of the moon;*
> *she comes nearer the earth than she was wont,*
> *and makes me mad.*
> —Shakespeare, *Othello*, Act V, Scene 2

Earlier this evening the Russian wolfhound who spends his nights on my porch was awakened by the full moon. It happened when a canine up the road reminded him. First the neighbor dog felt the silvery pull. Then, for several minutes, the two traded moonsongs. It is no wonder. Outside, on the brick porch, the light lay in watery blue pools. It is awfully difficult on the dogs. It made it impossible for me to be at rest.

I don't know what the dogs feel in the unmerciful moonlight. In evening the earth is supposed to turn its back on the light. Yet, here it is, bathing the porch in a blue obtrusiveness. It confuses the dogs. It has lifted me from my sleep.

The symbolic significance of the moon has always been wide in scope and complex in function. Cicero thought that moonlight contributed to the growth of plants and animals. Ancient Greenlanders believed that all celestial bodies were once human beings, but the moon in particular was accused of inciting people to orgies. It was for this reason they were prohibited from looking directly at the full moon.

Charles Darwin reasoned that since animal life originated in the watery deep, this lesson of the rhythmic tides was imprinted on all life that moves upon the earth, knitting us together in a common ancestry. Whatever the reason, we are bound together by universal threads of sympathy, and it is the moon that seems responsible as man and dog sit brooding in a wistful discomfort. It is enough to make both desire the darkness.

This evening, around midnight, after the dogs had shared their moonsong, I went out on the porch. The boxwoods smelled musty, my toes curled on the cold of the orange brick. By then, the wolfhound had sung himself to sleep. He left me awake to do the thinking.

I decided, while staring at the sleeping dog, that were it not for the neighbors—those who don't have dogs—I might have howled right along with the wolfhound and his chum. I think a man should get in a good howling among the boxwood every now and again. Even if it's just a loud moan. It's good for the man, and it makes the dog think his companion is trustworthy.

Eventually I returned to my sleep. The blue light stretched across the floor and emptied into my bed. I dreamed I was a feral child, grimy-faced with fierce bright eyes. I roamed with a pack of wolves, among strange, foreboding landscapes. At 3:12 a.m., the whistle atop the volunteer fire department a few miles away tore me from the dream. The aquamarine rays of the clock radio mingled with the moonlight. The wolfhound was awake on the porch, making the whistle a duet. I walked outside, without bothering to cover myself. The dog, nose pointed north like the arrow of a compass, was howling for all he was worth.

Standing among the boxwood in that dangerous blue light, I turned my face toward the heavens, filled my lungs with cool night air, and returned the favor in the key of C.

*October, 1987*

# As the Crickets' Chorus Fades

> *Further in the Summer than the Birds*
> *Pathetic from the Grass*
> *A minor Nation celebrates*
> *Its unobtrusive Mass.*
> —Emily Dickinson

This is the stillest of nights—starless and bible-black. There is a small, sweet breeze from the north. It brings the fading scent of roses. The last petals, the yellow ones, fade like summer hopes, but they seem to smell sweetest just before they fall. The grass is the color of avocados, and feels wet beneath my bare feet.

In a few weeks, it will turn the color of tow-headed boys grown old. There will be a few more nights like this, and then the fall will come in earnest.

In Indian summer the night still contains life. But it is hidden deep within the boxwood. There is a high-pitched half-sound made by a valiant "minor Nation" of crickets. Nature does its crumbling, its falling away. She gives us daily hints when we are not too busy to look, or at evening, to listen.

Each night, a few more voices have dropped from the boxwood chorus until now there are only a few. The fall's lapse into solitude is gradual. It is completed some time around the grading of first exams. By then, shoes must be worn. I can allot no time to summer's passing. I will not stop to hear the arrival of silence.

The school year has run headlong into the future: exams, papers, meetings, vacations, graduations, with no glance back in the direction of the crickets. We have moved swiftly, inexorably past a collection of moments for which we did not stop.

But tonight the crickets are still chirping. Their song is not a mournful one. It is sung by creatures whom God has not bothered with thoughts of the end. Only we have the capacity to discern that a few more grains of sand have fallen irretrievably through the hourglass. Only we make poems about it.

In a few days, the night sky will provide a dark and seamless background. The vacant sky will bring out the tender colors of life in all their purity. It is a time when looking at the sky forces us to envelop back upon ourselves, like the strange but noble self-referential paradoxes we are. The autumn sky will stand ready for contemplation. But I will be too busy to look.

And so it is this evening, while there is still time, the night is full of farewells. In the fading sound of the crickets, this night is like a sacrament. There is a fleeting grandeur, a fragile tranquility. It is a night, it is an Indian summer, that will never come again.

*October, 1987*

# Snow and the Best of Baltimore

I am sitting at home enjoying my new furniture. It is really quite attractive, though it might properly be called "early bachelor eclectic." It was after last week's snowstorm that I acquired the various kitchen chairs, a floor lamp, lawn chairs, a small bar, a couple of new metal trash cans and the coffee table on which my typewriter now sits.

I used to believe snow brought out the worst in Baltimoreans. Though I was born and raised here, I was educated in New England and northern Scotland, where even the sheep occasionally get goose flesh. Snow and bad weather are understood there as among the unalterable givens of the natural environment. In Baltimore the falling of snow engenders a pervading attitude that white fluffy precipitation of any amount is akin to nuclear fallout.

"Snow emergency plans" are invoked, schools close, public transportation halts, the Parkville Elks cancel their trip to Atlantic City. The city comes to a white stop.

The only activity that can be counted on in a Baltimore snowfall is the buying up of all available bread and milk as yet uncontaminated by the gamma rays. All my former experiences of Baltimoreans and snow consists of mental snapshots of short-tempered people waiting in supermarket lines with baskets filled to the top with toilet paper. Their faces tell of a collective fear more properly found in a government store in Siberia.

One must buy all one can, for there is the terrifying possibility another shipment will not arrive before the spring thaw.

When I used to think of snow in my hometown, I conjured up images of disgruntled motorists honking like deranged geese at an elderly woman whose car had decided to do its dying in the white-turned-to-gray slush. But the last snowfall has brought with it a new attitude fostered, I should think, by the acquisition of the new furniture.

I no longer view snow-plagued Baltimoreans as ill-tempered and selfish neurotics. When I came out of my house last week, I discovered, much to my delight, that several of my more benevolent neighbors had shoveled clean a number of parking spaces up and down the street, so that I might more easily park my car when I return after a difficult day of teaching.

They also left the various pieces of furniture and household items mentioned above. They were very neatly placed, individually, one or two for each parking space. Mine is a very close-knit neighborhood, which perhaps explains the widespread knowledge of my real need of furniture, and particularly of the trash cans. I suspect they may have been told by the mailman, or possibly the little man who reads my gas meter.

I no longer have any doubt. Snow brings out the best in Baltimoreans.

*February, 1987*

# He Who Plants Trees

*He who plants trees loves others besides himself.*
—English Proverb

I leave my house every morning about 7:15. These days the air is crisp and clean. It is like the cool rush that comes with inhaling a eucalyptus cough drop. But there is also in the air an unsuspected sharpness accompanied by a quickening in the breast, a deep sadness and a longing that signals departure.

When I leave in the morning, the sun is but a few moments old. It struggles to melt first frost from the windshield before I turn the key. In those few moments before I succumb again, before I put rubber on the road, notes on the lectern, questions in perspective, philosophers in their historical context, I stop to talk to the old dog on the porch. He still wags his tail and presses his narrow rib cage affectionately against my leg.

It is just about at that moment that I also engage in a ritual discussion about the weather with the gardener who works on the property. He has seen eighty-seven autumns like this one. His nearly toothless grin is only slightly less appreciative than the ancient wolfhound's greeting.

Each morning the gardener and I use the same sentences we employed this time last year. We talk about frost and pumpkins, dying roses and frozen soil. We have used these words together many autumns before. Mornings have turned mysteriously to months, months to seasons, seasons have turned to lifetimes. The words are part of a small island of permanence not easily washed away in the rivers of nature and chance.

I know the gardener cannot live forever, but I want him to. I seem only to let myself think about *it* when summer is busy doing its dying. There is something about the fall that turns our thoughts to all that is fragile. In early October, we all become practitioners of anticipatory grief. Today, although autumn is not yet golden, there is in the air a whispering of the end. Like the gardener, the very last of summer moves now at the slowest of measures, something close to an adagio for strings.

Earlier this evening, when I walked in the garden, I remembered that the old man's fingerprints are pressed deeply into every inch of this property's soil. Saplings now loom above the house, boxwood has grown thick and fragrant with decades of his care. The gardener's roses have had far more birthdays than I.

In the morning we will say our autumn words again, as if for the first time: "Winter is coming...not much summer left..." The old man will end the conversation by telling me I must take very good care of myself. I always respond by saying, "And you...and you."

In his essay "On Old Age," Cicero puts in the mouth of the aging Scipio a small soliloquy:

> I am wise in that I follow that good guide nature; it is not likely that when she has written the rest of the play, that she would, like a lazy playwright, skimp on the last act. There must be an ending, just as the crops and fruits come in the course of time to a period of fall. No wise man will resent this.

The gardener is unaware that he lives Cicero's ideal. This planter of trees prefers bible stories to Roman stoicism. He is particularly fond of the parable of the sowers and the seed.

To know how to grow old is the master work of wisdom. It is not so easy for most of us. But for this one old man, it is about as difficult as tending a garden.

*October, 1989*

# Music is its Roar

*He that will learn to pray,
let him go to the sea.*
—Scottish proverb

*Bethany Beach, Delaware*

It is not often I have a genuine sense of place, an experience of something fine and good that comes solely from where I am, not what or who I have become. There are many forms of homelessness. I am lucky enough to suffer, only intermittently, from the metaphysical variety.

I sit this evening on a small wooden porch that juts out above the dune line. The clumps of sea grass dotting mounds of white dune sand, like stubborn tufts of hair on a bald man's head, can no longer be seen. Earlier in the day, when the sun was high, I watched as a pair of four-year-old boys, looking like small King Canutes, threw wads of wet sand at the on-rushing surf. Just a little farther off shore, about ten yards apart, porpoises broke the surface almost simultaneously—one, two, three, four, five, then gone again. Thirty seconds later, they reappeared, noses and dorsal fins surfacing first, followed by a great arching and five choreographed dives into one disappearance.

But this evening everything has disappeared. I write with the aid of a small oil lamp found while rummaging in the kitchen. The lamp provides just enough light to see the paper's faint blue lines which run parallel to the invisible horizon.

Stretched out before me is a blackness that cannot be found in the city. Beyond the dunes, beyond the crickets sounding like the monotonous hum of high tension wires, at the very edge of the earth, the sea unfolds and then slowly gathers itself in again. The slowly building cadence, followed by a sudden crashing, is like no other sound. This evening, while my family sleeps and I am alone, no metaphor seems worthy of it.

I have been here now for nearly an hour, thinking and listening. A moment ago, I remembered a line from Byron that has started me writing. He speaks of "a society where none intrudes by the deep sea, and music is its roar." They are words written at night, by the sea.

Tomorrow the newspapers, once again, will bring me the world of men: a war waiting to happen in the middle east, rising gasoline prices, a late baseball game played on another coast. But this evening, the great sea drowns out all in its wide sound. The noise cleanses me. It imposes a rhythm upon everything. In the darkness, it seems to make the spiritual possible.

Ancient Hindu priests depicted the merging of individual souls with ultimate reality, Brahma, as drops splashing in a giant sea. The sound they made, it was said, was like a great wave crashing. Charles Darwin thought our deep fascination with the sea comes from a kind of racial memory of our oceanic origins, a time before we had set out to conquer the land and each other.

In a few days, back in the city, my students will bring clean spiral notebooks and freshly sharpened number-two pencils into my classroom. They and I, once again, will be very diligent. We will read together works by Plato, Aristotle, and Seneca, all men who loved the sea.

In one of my lectures, just before the trees on campus give up their leaves for dead, I will loosen my tie and speak earnestly about Plato's conception of immortality. And then I will tell them about this evening, and about how, just beyond the darkness, with a starless night and a cool breeze blowing from the west, the sea sounded like eternity.

*August, 1990*

# Politics

*A politician: one who would circumvent God.*
　　—WILLIAM SHAKESPEARE

# Why Did We Drop the Second Bomb?

*I hope for some part of peace—but I fear that machines are ahead of morals by some centuries and when morals catch up perhaps there will be no reason for any of it.*
—Harry S. Truman, July 16, 1945

At 11:02 a.m. on August 9, 1945, a blinding flash of amethyst colored light cut sharply across the Nagasaki sky. It was followed an instant later by a blast of searing heat and a rumbling sound like distant thunder. A second violent rush of burning air followed, even more intense than the first. Then came a complicated series of shattering noises, like the sound of a million pieces of glass disintegrating simultaneously. In the western sky, a monstrous mushroom cloud had formed. The lower part, the stem, acted more like the tail of a tornado, pulling things up into the body of the cloud. The shape and color of the ominous mushroom continued to shift for the next few moments until it finally dissipated into a strange black rain that covered anything still standing with black soot and radioactive material.

Directly beneath the epicenter, the damage was enormous, despite the fact the bomb had not struck near the intended point. Everything within a half-mile circle was completely vaporized. Steel beams liquefied; all living things in that circle of death were completely incinerated. The bombing of Nagasaki had come three days after the leveling of Hiroshima, a city of 300,000 people, to the south. On August 9, by 11:03 a.m., half of Nagasaki's

50,000 buildings and 40,000 of its citizens were gone. By 1980, another 30,000 lives would be claimed by the black soot and its aftermath.

Nagasaki had not been the primary target that August morning of 1945. The B-29 bomber that carried the plutonium bomb, nicknamed "Fatman" after Winston Churchill, had approached Kokura, the arsenal city, shortly after 9:00 a.m. But when Captain Kermit Beahan, the bombardier, looked through his bombsight, all he saw were clouds of thick smoke, the by-product of a conventional attack on the Yawata steel factory staged two days earlier by General Curtis Lemay. After two more unsuccessful passes over Kokura, Major Charles Sweeney headed "Bock's Car," the plane preempted from Captain Fred Bock, in the direction of Nagasaki.

One set of questions about the events of August of 1945 that remains, despite forty-seven years of discussion and debate, is why the United States chose to drop two bombs. These queries are made more complicated by the realization that Secretary of War Henry Stimson, on the morning of August 8, had awakened President Harry Truman with a set of photographs of the destruction of Hiroshima. The complete annihilation of the city could be seen quite clearly in pictures. Stimson also gave the president a detailed report, prepared by the Strategic Air Force, on the damage. Stimson indicated that it might be possible to secure a Japanese surrender without the detonation of the second bomb. But the plans to drop that second bomb were not halted.

Prior to the attack on Hiroshima a strong consensus had developed among policymakers that the only alternative to the use of the atomic bomb was a land invasion that was sure to cost hundreds of thousands of American lives. Very few challenged this assumption at the time. Mr. Truman was to use it until his death in 1972 in defense of his decision to drop both bombs. Ironically, reports of Japanese peace feelers from early August quickly surfaced a few days after V-J day. The United States Strategic Bombing survey, after a year's worth of interviews with high-ranking Japanese military officials, in December, 1946, published a report suggesting that Japan would have surrendered by December of 1945, and probably by November, even without the use of atomic weapons. The reasoning of the writers of the survey went like this:

> By July, 1945, Japan's economic system had been shattered. Production of civilian goods was below the level of subsistence. Munitions output had been curtailed to less than half the wartime peak, a level that could not support sustained military operations against our forces. The economic basis of Japanese resistance had been destroyed.

Mr. Truman, immediately following the dropping of the first bomb, announced that: "The world would note the first atomic bomb was dropped on Hiroshima, a military base. That is because we wished the first attack to avoid, insofar as possible, the killing of civilians." Although it is true that Hiroshima was a major port and the regional military headquarters, there were also over 60,000 civilians incinerated along with the military personnel of the Second Army complex on the shoulder of Mount Futaba. Mr. Truman was fully aware of the destruction the first bomb had wrought. Why did he do nothing about the planned use of the second bomb?

Until quite recently, the evidence available to historians for determining President Truman's thinking about the dropping of the two bombs had been circumstantial and sketchy at best. James Byrne, Truman's Secretary of State, had suggested we use both bombs before the Soviet Union, who had entered the war against Japan shortly after midnight on August 9, could "get in so much on the kill." A number of revisionist historians, using Stimson's diaries, have argued that Stimson saw the use of the bombs as a "master card" for dealing with the post-war Soviets. What these revisionist historians have failed to realize is that there are really two claims that need to be kept separate. First, did Truman wish to keep the Russians out of the war? And second, were the bombs used on Hiroshima and Nagasaki a "master card" in dealing with the Soviets after the war?

In 1979 a collection of handwritten notes made by Truman in the weeks preceding August, 1945, were found at the Truman Library. In July, 1945, Truman had attended the Big Three Summit meeting in Potsdam, just outside of Berlin. After hearing of the successful test detonation in Los Alamos, New Mexico, on July 16, Mr. Truman wrote the following in his diary:

> I hope for some sort of peace—but I fear that machines are ahead of morals by some centuries and when morals catch up perhaps there will be no reason for any of it.

On July 17, Josef Stalin informed Truman of his desire to overthrow the Franco regime in Spain. Truman called Stalin's suggestion "dynamite." In the diary, he adds: "But I have some dynamite too which I'm not exploding now." Truman also made several references to the reaffirmation of an agreement Stalin had made earlier: "[Stalin will] be in the Jap war on August 15th." To this Truman added, "*Finis* Japs when that comes about."

On the following day, July 18, the president wrote a letter to Bess Truman. This letter, as well as others sent from Potsdam, were discovered among Mrs. Truman's papers in 1983:

> I have gotten what I came for—Stalin goes to war on August 15 with no strings attached... I'll say that we'll end the war a year sooner now and think of the kids who won't be killed!

The implications of these new sources should be clear. As late as July, 1945, Truman believed the entry of the Soviets into the Pacific war would end the conflict before an invasion of Japan the following Fall was necessary.

If Truman believed the entry of the Soviet Union into the war was sufficient to bring the conflict to a close, why did he drop not only one bomb, but two? The answer may be that both Mr. Stimson and the revisionists are half right. The new evidence seems to disprove the revisionist contention that Truman did not want the Russians in the war. In another letter to Bess Truman, dated July 18, the president describes a tough meeting with Stalin and Churchill. At the end of the letter, Mr. Truman tells his wife of his goal: "I want the Jap war won and I want them both in it." At the same time, the new evidence also suggests that the two bombs were used, as some revisionists suggest, "as much against the Russians as the Japanese."

The victims of Hiroshima and Nagasaki do not use this kind of metaphorical language.

*August, 1987*

# Done in the Style of Double-T

I was deeply ensconced the other afternoon in the advertising supplement of our local community paper. The truth is: a friend gave it to me. Like my attitude toward vitamins, my view of advertising is that I generally get the recommended daily adult dosage without resorting to supplements.

I was given the advertising supplement because it contained a feature article on the Double-T Diner, a Catonsville landmark for the past three decades. During my high school years the diner became an obligatory stop on the way home from a variety of activities my parents didn't generally want me engaging in.

Six or eight of us boys, for example, would attend the drive-in movies for the price of two—using various means of deception. Afterwards, we would travel to the diner to consume enormous waffles that hung over the sides of our plates, or stacks of buttermilk pancakes served any time of day or night.

The place was always filled with truck drivers, beehive hairdos and people who crowded into the chrome and glass leviathan for a good meal, without a side order of fanciness.

Now, twenty years later, I still go to the diner a few times a month. It has always been the sort of place that's good for your nerves, for it's somehow managed to hoodwink history.

Outside the glass doors of the Double-T the civilized world was turning into plastic food served in plastic boxes, but inside the diner you could still find a real hamburger and an Elvis tune on the small juke boxes in every booth.

For over thirty years the Double-T has been one of those architectural anomalies. It was so incredibly unattractive as a structure it transcended ugliness to the point of taking on a kind of mystical beauty—a Platonic form of the diner sitting amidst gasoline stations, establishments engaged in the sale of kitchen tile, and automobile dealerships.

But the winds of change seem to be blowing at the intersection of Rolling Road and Route 40. The new owners of the diner, Tom, John and Lou Korologris, have decided to fix up the Double-T. As Jeff Benjamin, the writer of the feature, explained: "The outside will be dressed up well. Forget that shiny chrome stuff. It will be replaced by stone..."

Later he added, "It's amazing what $350,000 can do when you are looking to shave the beard off a thirty-year-old landmark."

I found all this puzzling and deeply disturbing—the kind of reaction I might have to someone putting a pair of double-knit trousers on Michelangelo's David. But then I read the remainder of the article. The end of Benjamin's feature not only contained the answer to why three apparently intelligent men would want to ruin the looks of a perfectly good diner, but it also offered a possible solution to a much larger political dilemma regarding a perfectly good used governor's mansion—the one in Annapolis being renovated by Governor William Donald Schaefer and the state's First Friend, Hilda Mae Snoops.

At the end of Benjamin's piece, he quotes Janet Hare, a waitress at the diner for the past twenty-six years: "This place must be all right," she said. "[Schaefer] comes in here to eat... That's right. He came in here when he was mayor and he comes in here now."

This seemingly off-hand remark may go a long way toward explaining the Korologris' decision to make over their restaurant. They have become so impressed by the governor and his trips to their diner that they are attempting to make him feel at home by turning the building into a replica of the governor's mansion.

But we may also have in Hare's remark the key to understanding the architectural and interior design tastes of Schaefer and Snoops. The governor has become so fond of the Double-T Diner, he's having the mansion in Annapolis redone in the style of his favorite restaurant on Route 40.

To paraphrase Benjamin, it's amazing what $1 million of the taxpayers' money and private donations can do when you are looking to shave off the beard of a recently restored Maryland landmark.

*October, 1989*

# Say It Again, Dan

*News Item:*
*Vice President Dan Quayle, in an exchange of letters with American Samoa's representative in Congress, has sought to clear up his mystifying reference to Samoans as "happy campers."*

*Some Samoans complained that Quayle's remark, made during a brief stop in Pago Pago last month, had "patronizing and condescending connotations," wrote Eni F.H. Falemavaega, the territory's non-voting delegate in the House...*

*Quayle made matters worse by mispronouncing Pago Pago "Pogo Pogo," like the comic strip, which "caused some to question whether [he was], again, ridiculing the Samoan people," the delegate wrote.*

Dear Mr. Vice President:

There seems to have been some terrible mix-up last month. After talking with your press secretary early in April, I rounded up all the residents here in the swamp. They were very anxious to talk with you about some environmental issues.

I even invited some of the vacationers from the campsites nearby. They all said they were very happy about your visit.

You can imagine our disappointment when you didn't show. The alligators were particularly unhappy. Several experienced swamp-lag swimming all that way to meet you. They said there's a good chance they'll never vote Republican again. Some of the other opossums have even started asking if I might run for vice president next time.

One of the campers said he read in the papers that you were in Samoa the day you were supposed to be here. This didn't make him, or the rest of the campers, very happy.

What gives?

Willing to give you another chance if you have a good explanation,

                                     Pogo

*May, 1989*

# Goals

*An article on February 1, 1986, by John Agresto, then acting director of the National Endowment for the Humanities, expressed the Reagan administration view that racial and sexual goals in hiring and promotion are "odious." This article was in reply.*

John Agresto's remarks about the unfairness of affirmative action programs seem a bit like Jerry Falwell writing to Jimmy Swaggart for the purpose of persuading him to praise the Lord. There is little to be accomplished in preaching to the already converted. Perhaps it is better to understand Agresto's comments as aimed not at the Equal Employment Opportunity Commission, but rather at those recalcitrant individuals who are perceived by the Reagan administration as reverse discriminators.

Throughout his article, Agresto suggests that, as a nation, we must soon make a choice between whether we will adhere to the principle that race and sex should not be factors considered in the hiring and promotion of people in this country, or whether we will continue to hire and promote just because a particular individual happens to be Black or female.

Agresto refers to this issue as "a simple moral question: Should anyone be preferred or held back because of race or sex?" His answer, of course, is a resounding "No." "Blindness to a person's color or religion, gender or race was, we thought, the hallmark of civilized justice."

To say the least, all this is an exercise in lofty rhetoric, but a rhetoric that conceals a very real, and perhaps dangerous, confusion.

The confusion becomes more readily understandable when we rephrase Agresto's apparent dichotomy: Where minorities and women have been clearly under-represented in the work force, do we have a moral responsibility as a nation, and as individual citizens, for the hiring and promotion of qualified Blacks and females? The answer is clearly "Yes." In situations where qualified minorities and women are hired it is not *just* because they are Black or female. It is because they are good candidates for those jobs, and because their hiring or promotion helps in a small but important way to make ours a more just society.

Agresto's confusion is further displayed in his failure to understand the very important distinction between individual justice and compensatory justice. Plato's definition of justice involving "getting what one is due" has remained without serious critics for the last 2,500 years. But it is important to keep in mind that the receivers of justice are not always individual citizens. In a just society, there may also be certain classes or segments of society who, as a group, have not received their fair share. These people must be compensated.

Compensatory justice can be done by hiring members of the slighted segments of society. In our nation, those groups certainly include Blacks and women. In an ideal situation, however, hiring well-qualified women and highly competent minorities promotes individual justice and compensatory justice at the same time. The real responsibility, then, for the government, as well as for its individual citizens, is to search for well-qualified minorities and women—people who may allow us as a nation to achieve both individual and compensatory justice.

Nowhere in Agresto's remarks does he entertain the possibility that individual and compensatory justice could be promoted simultaneously. He seems to assume the only real reason for the hiring of Blacks and women is their color or sex. Perhaps that tells us more about the need for affirmative action programs in which competent minorities and women are hired than Agresto and the Reagan administration in general wish to know.

*February, 1986*

# How to Solve the Congressional Pay-Raise Dilemma

Both houses of Congress must decide in the next few weeks whether they will veto a presidential order granting them a raise from their current $77,000-a-year salary to a proposed $89,500. If the vote is not taken in the House and Senate, the increase becomes automatic.

The order also provides raises for about 3,000 other high-ranking government employees, including the vice president and federal judges.

It comes after an earlier suggestion that congressional salaries be increased to $115,000 received less than enthusiastic support from a variety of quarters.

A recent ABC television poll showed 95% of Americans opposed a raise for members of Congress. So if congressmen fail to veto the order, they are essentially acting in their own self-interest but against the will of their constituents. (They receive a cost-of-living raise anyway.)

The other evening I watched as Ted Koppel refereed a debate between Ralph Nader and former Tennessee Senator Howard Baker on the issue of the salary increase. There was something amusing about watching Koppel, a man with a reported salary of $900,000 per annum, asking probing questions of the consumer advocate and the former Senate majority leader.

From what I can gather, Baker was in favor of the proposed raise because of the enormous burden of keeping two houses—one in Washington and the other in the congressman's home state. For the past few days I have been thinking about how difficult it must be for members of Congress to leave an empty house behind like that. It's a financial burden, not to mention the worry that must go with leaving one's house unattended for long periods of time.

I think I may have a solution. It may help not only with that problem, but it could also assist in some small way in solving the dilemma of the homeless in America.

It is this: While congressional members are busy in Washington making laws, increasing the defense budget and raising the national debt, back in their home states homeless people could be moved into the vacant houses of senators and congressmen.

The proposed increase of $12,500 could then be given to these formerly homeless people to run their new houses. Half of the money could be returned to members of Congress in the form of rent. The remaining $6,250 could be used by the new occupants for food and clothing.

There are 535 members of Congress. If the average American family consists of four people, this gives us space for 2,140 homeless individuals. Meanwhile, with a 3% cost-of-living raise, plus $528 a month from the rent of their formerly vacant houses, each member of Congress would net an extra $720 per month.

The president should sign an order making this new plan effective in a couple of weeks. I think it should happen automatically unless the homeless people veto the idea.

*January, 1987*

# Supreme Court Joins the Blood-Revenge Crowd

In two separate decisions involving the death penalty, the Supreme Court last week gave clear indication it will not stand in the way of a widespread national desire to practice blood revenge under the grim guise of justice.

In the first case, the court ruled by a 5-4 margin that capital punishment may be imposed not only on first-degree murderers, but also on the killers' accomplices. The new ruling makes it possible for accomplices to be capitally tried for murders they did not actually commit, and where they had no intention to kill.

The court suggested the test for whether a criminal should be put to death is not the traditional notion of criminal responsibility and evil intent, but rather a murkier standard it called "reckless indifference to human life." The court did not, however, supply criteria for how we might know when this new condition is met. On the face of it, one can think of a whole host of characters in political and military circles who might now qualify for the death penalty.

One of the baffling elements—and there are many—regarding this first ruling is that Justice Byron White voted with the majority on the "reckless indifference to human life" standard. In 1982 the same White wrote an eloquent opinion in which he stressed that capital punishment should only be imposed on those who have had "causal responsibility" for a first-degree murder, or where there was a clear intention that the murder take place.

It came as no real surprise that the new Reagan-appointed judges sided with Chief Justice William Rehnquist and Justice Lewis Powell in their majority decision to broaden the scope of existing capital punishment statutes. And Justices Brennan, Marshall, Blackmun and Stevens, voicing their strong minority objections, could have been predicted. But White's new view suggests he may be suffering from an advanced form of judicial amnesia, a pernicious and dangerous disease. Its two chief symptoms are a bad memory and a sometimes reckless indifference to human life.

The second of the court's decisions last week was at least equally disturbing, for it points to an unwillingness on the part of the same five judges to consider clear and overwhelming evidence that the death penalty is used in this country in a racially discriminatory way.

In fact, it was the specter of selective prosecution and discrimination that led the court in 1972 to rule that the death penalty as practiced was unconstitutional. In 1972 the court heard evidence which showed that, of the 3,863 persons executed in the U.S. since 1930, 2,006 were Black. Of 455 people executed for rape during the same period, 405 were Black, and all but two of those were in southern states.

A careful, well-reasoned approach to these figures led the 1972 court to conclude:

> Finally there is evidence that the imposition of the death sentence and the exercise of dispensing power by the courts and the executive follow discriminatory patterns. The death penalty is disproportionately imposed and carried out on the poor, the Negro, and the members of unpopular causes.

In the same ruling the court expressed optimism that more careful and clear-headed sentencing procedures by states would prevent arbitrary discrimination in the future.

Since 1976, the year the Supreme Court reinstated capital punishment, seventy people have died at the hands of the state. Of the forty who were Black, thirty-nine had killed white people. Seventy percent of all people now sitting on death row have killed whites. Murderers of whites are four times more likely to be executed than the killers of Blacks. If the perpetrator is Black and the victim is white, the murderer is twenty-two times more likely to be executed than the white killers of white victims.

Despite this evidence, which was presented before the court last week, Rehnquist, White, O'Connor, Powell and Scalia upheld Georgia's death penalty law. Since 1976, in Georgia, only Blacks have been executed. Justice Powell, who wrote the majority opinion, discussed this anomaly: "We decline to assume that what is unexplained is invidious."

Powell may be correct when he points out there is something "unexplained" in these two rulings, or perhaps it is something that is just not readily admitted. Thurgood Marshall argued in the 1972 decision that as soon as the public was educated about the lack of effectiveness of the death penalty as a deterrence, only people with a strong sense of retribution would continue to support the death penalty. Today that spirit of retribution, that desire for blood revenge, has captured the hearts of most Americans.

It has also captured the minds of five Supreme Court Justices. It makes little difference to them that revenge seems most desired when the victims are white and the murderers are Black. Some 2,500 years ago, Plato made an important distinction between retributive justice and distributive justice—justice meted out fairly. He thought the former was useless unless the latter was kept in mind.

The Supreme Court would do well to consider that distinction. Justice, not revenge, should be blind.

*February, 1988*

# A Proper Guest List

I know it is not my place to talk about women's issues. Every time I begin to talk about women's issues, one of my female colleagues will screw her mouth up in a look of profound disgust and say something like, "You know, that's a women's issue, and you really have no right talking about it." Of course I know she is right, so ordinarily I try to refrain from talking about women's issues, but the other day one popped up in the news and I'm just dying to talk about it.

It all began when I read that Pamela Harriman, the widow of W. Averell Harriman, former U.S. ambassador to the Soviet Union, was asked by Soviet officials to invite five prominent American women to have tea with Raissa Gorbachev.

Since the tea last Thursday, Harriman has taken quite a bit of heat about the selections (reportedly made in consultation with Liana Dubinin, wife of the Soviet ambassador): Senator Barbara A. Mikulski, D-Md.; Supreme Court Justice Sandra Day O'Connor; University of Chicago president Hanna Gray; and Washington Post chairman Katharine Graham.

Most of the criticism, at least from what I can divine from news accounts, came from representatives of leading women's groups. The spokeswomen all had their mouths screwed up in that same look of profound disgust my colleague has when she is about to tell me that something I am talking about is a women's issue and I should mind my own business.

Representatives from the National Organization for Women and the National Women's Political Caucus pointed out that all of the selections were white and from the social elite, and thus were hardly a real cross-section of American females.

It would be very difficult to sidestep this criticism. But rather than Harriman screwing up her mouth in profound disgust and doing battle with various national women's organizations—after all, she only gave the tea at the Soviet's request—she should simply have another party, and try to get it right this time.

Of course narrowing down the guest list would be nearly as difficult as it was the first time, for we have only eliminated the original five invitees of 80 million or so adult American women. But since I'm not supposed to talk about women's issues anyway, and since I may never get another opportunity, let me offer the following as a possible short list for the new soiree: Aunt Jemima, Zsa Zsa Gabor, Miss Piggy, Chiquita Banana and Anita Bryant.

I know at first glance this isn't a very impressive list, but before you screw your mouth up in profound disgust, remember these important things:

First, the invitation is for breakfast. Aunt Jemima could bring the pancakes, Anita Bryant the orange juice, Chiquita Banana the fruit for the cereal. And Zsa Zsa could bring the champagne. Miss Piggy would be asked to give of herself for the breakfast, but if she agreed, she would be making the ultimate sacrifice for her country. If American bacon doesn't impress Raissa under those circumstances, what will?

A second clear benefit of the new guest list is its great diversity: one Black woman, one eastern European immigrant who likes to stay home, one conservative Republican, one representative of the animal kingdom and one member of the Hispanic community whose corporate home is in Cincinnati.

Of course, the Reagan administration's Department of Immigration and Naturalization will want to make sure that Chiquita Banana is really a citizen, so we'd need to have a few substitutes on call. Minnie Mouse would be good. She's from the entertainment industry. Minnie Pearl might be even better. We'd make her keep the price tag on her hat. That would really show Raissa we are committed to capitalism.

If anyone asks you where you heard all this, don't give her my name. I want none of the blame, nor will I take any of the credit. I'm not supposed to talk about women's issues.

*December, 1987*

# Dogs without Heroes

For the past two weeks I have been very concerned about the mental health of the Russian wolfhound who lives at my house. He has always been active, loyal and extremely well-adjusted—the kind of dog who, seeing me make a fool of myself, not only will not scold me, but also will enthusiastically make a fool of *himself*.

But this summer he really has not been himself. At first I chalked it up to the Baltimore weather, which in July and August hangs over the city like a giant plastic bag, trapping the intense heat and humidity within. I thought the weather, hard enough on human beings, was enough to place even the most well-adjusted wolfhound into a profound funk.

Last week I began to develop another theory. It came to me all at once during a break in the Iran-contra hearings. In the commercial, a dim-witted dog harnessed to a miniature chuck wagon paraded across the screen.

I think the Russian wolfhound is depressed because the contemporary American dog has no real role models. These days there are no canine heroes the average dog can emulate.

Dogs growing up twenty-five years ago were surrounded by heroic figures. But that was when dogs were dogs, if you know what I mean. Roy Rogers' dog, Bullet; Rin Tin Tin; Lassie, a female dog who was too busy to watch soap operas or Iran-contra hearings; Sergeant Preston of the Yukon's dog, King: all were dogs a puppy could want to grow up to become.

These days, a tender, impressionable dog has few role models from which to choose. There is the pathetic pooch with the chuck wagon dragging behind, and that wimpy dog, Benji, who in fifteen years of making movies still can't keep the hair out of his eyes.

Lately we have all seen beer advertisements featuring an ugly spotted dog named Spuds MacKenzie. In his commercials, Spuds waddles around in a tuxedo, like an anorexic pig trying to look important. Rin Tin Tin didn't need to wear his uniform to impress people, or other dogs for that matter. It is hard to imagine Ol' Yeller allowing himself to be tied to a chuck wagon.

The thing that is really depressing the Russian wolfhound is a rumor he saw in last week's tabloids—*Spuds MacKenzie is pregnant*. I tried cheering up the dog by showing him Quickdraw McGraw reruns. It did no good. He has decided the American canine community is devoid of authentic heroes.

The past few weeks, in between thinking about the welfare of the Russian wolfhound, I've been watching the Iran-contra hearings. The dog has been watching with me. I think he has decided that he is not the only species having trouble finding legitimate heroes these days. Rin Tin Tin wore no medals on his chest.

*July, 1987*

# The Tragedy of Marion Barry

*The climax of every tragedy lies
in the deafness of its hero.*
—Albert Camus, *The Rebel*

At its best, tragedy reveals, simultaneously, in one complete action, a character's total possibilities, as well as his fatal limitations. All that he could and should do is graphically revealed to the audience. All that he does or fails to do spills out on the stage, as in the last scene of *Hamlet,* readily apparent even to those sitting in the last row.

The trial of Mayor Marion Barry reminds us that tragedy is not just to be found in ancient Athens or among the Elizabethans. Ours is an age of tragedy, tragedy in the classical sense, not just because our time is sadder and more dangerous than most, but because it is filled to the top with ambiguity, ambiguity of the moral kind.

In tragedy, moral ambiguity always brings fingerpointing: Tiresias, the blind soothsayer, reluctantly points to Oedipus, Oedipus blindly points back at the seer, while innocence and guilt revolve around the pair, whirling at such speed that the two become nearly indistinguishable.

In Marion Barry all of Aristotle's tragic elements are present: He begins the tale as a fighter for civil rights, a man a little nobler than the rest of us, who, even if sympathetic to the cause, preferred to watch from the safety of our living rooms; there is his recognition and reversal in grainy video tapes brought to the same living rooms nearly three decades later. One could hear the tragedy echoed in Barry's voice at that moment of recognition—there is nothing more tragic than the realization of the utter impossibility of changing what one has done: between the beginning and the end of the Barry drama, not just in the hero but in minor characters as well, we have seen a good bit of the requisite pride, the inerrant magnet constantly pointing in the direction of the self.

But as Albert Camus points out in his essay, "Neither Victims Nor Executioners," ours is an age where tragedy is collective. In the Barry case, tragedy plays itself out, not just in the courtroom, but in every corner of the District of Columbia, on front stoops and over backyard fences, in bars and social clubs, office buildings and taxi cabs. And wherever that collective tragedy can be found, moral ambiguity can be seen residing at its center.

In the collective tragedy, whites often point the finger at Blacks. They privately call them gullible, willing to believe anything if it is necessary to protect their pride. Just as frequently, Blacks point the finger back at whites, and at a justice system that seems to them long on justice that is retributive and far short of justice that is distributive.

In the collective tragedy neither side is blind. It is more like those perceptual puzzles where one sees a duck, while another sees a rabbit in the same picture. What is needed, to see the other side, is a kind of conversion. But that is precisely what is impossible in genuine tragedy. Richard Sewall once remarked that "no tragedy can tell the whole truth." In the collective tragedy that swirls around Marion Barry, we learn different truths. It seems we are incapable of conversion to a collective truth, perhaps the whole truth.

At the end of *Oedipus Rex,* the hero blinds himself and flees the city, taking the plague with him. In Washington, no matter what the verdict in this collective tragedy, one thing is clear: the plague will remain.

*July, 1990*

# Good & Evil

*As long as one believes that the evil man wears horns, one will not discover an evil man.*
—Erich Fromm

# Indissoluble Ties

*All reigns of terror are alike, all are of the same origin, you will not get me to distinguish between them. I have seen too much, I know men too well, and I am too old now. Fear disgusts me in everybody, and behind all the fine talk of those butchers, lies fear, and only fear. Massacres are due to fear; hate is but an alibi.*
—George Bernanos, *A Diary of My Times*

As I stand in a city park, shadows stretch across the wet earth. They lengthen and point east. I watch as panic is transmitted like bad news across a flock of pigeons pecking at cobblestones. The first gets a little nervous and takes to flight. In another instant the entire flock is wheeling in the air, heading east, as if the first had been tethered by some invisible cord to the rest of his kin. We humans are like these pigeons.

Farther off to the east a few *homo sapiens* become afraid of students demonstrating in a public square. The old men believe they must take some action against the fear. It lays hold of them, sinks its teeth deeply into the backs of their leathered necks. They must destroy the fear, so they kill the students.

In moral matters what begins in fear so often ends in wickedness. None of us is very good at naming the beast. In religion and politics, or when politics comes to look too much like religion, what starts in fear usually ends in fanaticism. Fear is comfortable as either principle or motive, but it is always the beginning of evil. What were once feudal children afraid of the dark have become old men in China afraid of the light.

The rest of us sit gape-eyed before our television sets, or read newspaper accounts that call the horror "unbelievable," "incomprehensible," as if we all have not come regularly to believe the unbelievable. Over our morning coffee we once again must comprehend the incomprehensible.

Here in the west a kind of moral amnesia sets in. It is replaced by China experts whose faces flash on the screen. They try to divine for us what the fearful old men will do next. The experts have been hired for the week to add scrutability to the inscrutable.

In the process, we forget we are tethered by invisible but indissoluble ties, not just to the dead students, but also to the old men with blood on their hands. There are knots we have tied in this phantom cord. They have been made by us, tied off with national guardsmen, fire hoses, police dogs, and young Chicago officers in riot gear. The knots were made at places with names shunted off to a siding of our conscience: Kent State, Birmingham, Selma, and Sowetto. It matters not how big or small the knots. What matters is that we have forgotten. "Memory," Rollo May tells us, "is not just the imprint of the past upon us; it is the keeper of what is meaningful for our deepest hopes and fears." What we choose to forget may tell us volumes more about our fears than that which we recall.

The China experts repeatedly tell us the massacre was committed by the Peoples' Army, as if there could be any other kind.

*May, 1989*

# The Meese Pornography Commission: Old Principles in New Clothing

A few weeks ago, the Justice Department, in response to recommendations from the Reagan administration Commission on Pornography and Obscenity headed by Attorney General Edwin Meese, III, announced its plans to form a special team for prosecution of the offenders of those statutes.

Along with the team of prosecutors, the Department of Justice also announced plans for the development of a national data base to serve as resource center or clearinghouse to be used by law enforcement agencies and prosecutors at the state and local levels.

These announcements came after a number of antipornography groups over the last few months have been very critical of the Justice Department's delay in responding to the Meese Commission's report issued in July of this year. The Commission criticized the Justice Department for what was seen as a failure to bring a substantial number of obscenity cases to trial in recent years. The Meese Commission report pointed out that between 1978 and the first half of 1986 only 100 people were indicted in the United States on charges of violating federal obscenity laws, and only seventy-one of those people were subsequently convicted.

However one question that lingers about the findings of the Meese Commission is why its recommendations contradict those of a 1970 Commission on Pornography and Obscenity formed during the Nixon administration. The Nixon Commission recommended the repeal of legislation prohibiting the sale of obscene materials to consenting adults. The 1970 Commission appears to have used the principle of harm as the measuring stick in its deliberations.

The Meese Commission's recommendations, however, included banning the sale of large numbers of pornographic materials to adults because it claimed a causal connection could be shown between certain sexually explicit materials and the committing of violent crimes. It would appear that the 1986 Commission also used the principle of harm in forming its recommendations, but it came to a different conclusion about the harmfulness of pornographic materials.

At no time since the publication of the Meese Commission's report has any member of the new Commission, nor in the Reagan administration, raised the question about the seeming contradiction in the findings of the two commissions. Until this discrepancy is satisfactorily explained, the appointment of the special team of prosecutors seems more than a little premature and perhaps ill-advised.

One way to understand the Reagan administration's willingness to move so quickly on the question of pornography, despite contradictory evidence suggested by the two presidential panels, is to see that the Meese Commission may not have been operating with the principle of harm at the center of its deliberations after all. The principle of harm, first stated by the nineteenth-century philosopher and social critic John Stuart Mill, states that conduct may be prohibited if it causes harm to others. That some other philosophical point of view may have been at the heart of the Meese Commission's report goes a long way in explaining why the 1986 Commission's findings have been so widely criticized by social scientists.

In spurning the 1970 report, President Nixon remarked, "American morality is not to be trifled with. As long as I am in the White House there will be no relaxation of government efforts to control and eliminate smut from our national life."

It is clear President Nixon rejected the earlier Commission's report not because of the principle of harm, but rather because he was employing what philosophers sometimes call the legal-moral principle. In its simplest form this principle states that conduct should be prohibited under the law if it is immoral. The legal-moral principle may well be the other unnamed philosophical point of view at work in the Meese Commission's report. In some ways, President Nixon may have been more honest about his underlying reasons for wanting to ban pornography than the members of the Meese Commission have been.

Like Mr. Nixon, the 1986 Commission with Mr. Meese as its head appears to have had the legal-moral principle at the center of its deliberations. Unlike Mr. Nixon, the Meese Commission has dressed that legal-moral principle up in new social scientific clothing so that it might be mistaken for the principle of harm.

One piece of evidence to support this claim comes from the Meese Commission itself. Last summer, while the Commission was still preparing its report, it sent a menacing letter to several chains of convenience stores, as well as other retail establishments, suggesting those businesses should stop the sale of *Playboy* and other similar magazines. This suggestion certainly was not made because the Commission had established a causal connection between buying a *Playboy* at the 7-11 and the committing of violent crimes.

What is perhaps ironic about the findings of both Commissions is that the most reasonable philosophical approach to the problem of pornography and obscenity lies not solely in the use of the principle of harm, nor in legal-moralism. The later may be too weak, while the former is certainly too strong.

The American Civil Liberties' position on pornography is essentially one that solely uses the principle of harm. In a pamphlet published by the ACLU, they point out: "The question in a case involving obscenity...is whether the words or pictures are used in such circumstances and are of such a nature as to create a clear and present danger."

In the view of the ACLU, literature, film, drama, painting and the print media are considered forms of expression subject to the same rules as any expression of opinion. Since no causal connection can be made between the viewing of pornography and a rise in violent crime, they argue, the publication and selling of pornography should be treated like any other case involving the freedom of expression or freedom of the press. As the ACLU reminds us, "Every act of deciding what should be banned carried with it a danger to the community."

This position would appear to be the preferred point of view on pornography and obscenity, until one is confronted with examples like that provided by Louis Schwartz in an article about pornography published in the *Columbia Law Review*. Professor Schwartz raises an interesting question about whether we should ban a rich homosexual from using a billboard in Time Square to promulgate the pleasures and techniques of sodomy. If the ACLU's notion of harm was applied in this case, it would be difficult to construct a rationale for banning the billboard, for no clear and present danger exists for those who might view it. Yet it would be just as difficult, even for the most committed advocate of freedom of expression, to condone the billboard.

What Schwartz's example points out is that in our everyday deliberations about pornography, it may be of real use to employ a third philosophical notion, the principle of offense, in conjunction with the principle of harm, to guide us in our assessment of pornography.

But Schwartz also points out that people sometimes take offense at the most inane and harmless things. This offense principle must therefore be used in such a way that it does not open the door to the wholesale and unwarranted banning suggested by the Meese Commission.

One way to assure undue suppression of materials would not occur is to use two measuring sticks in connection with the principle of offense: the reasonable-person standard and the standard of reasonable avoidability. The reasonable-person test applied to the billboard case would ask the question: Would a reasonable person be offended by the poster? The answer to that question is clearly yes. The second test in regard to the applicability of the offense principle is to ask if the billboard is reasonably avoidable? The answer to this query is probably not.

Schwartz and others have suggested that where something is universally offensive to the reasonable person, and where it is not easily avoidable, the state may have good reasons for prohibiting display of that material, despite the fact that it does not pose a "clear and present danger."

This simple two-part test, if applied to cases of pornography and obscenity, goes a long way in steering a middle path between the excesses of both the Meese Commission and those of the ACLU.

In the meantime, we await the appointment of the special team of prosecutors, realizing that a good deal more clear thinking needs to be done about the issue of pornography. Before the Justice Department empowers those prosecutors to act, it would seen reasonable to clarify why there is a discrepancy between the findings of the Nixon and Reagan Commissions on pornography. At the heart of that discrepancy one is not likely to find a disagreement about crime statistics. What one is likely to discover is the legal-moral principle masquerading as the principle of harm.

*December, 1986*

# Knowing a Good Man When We See One

*Never can true courage dwell with them, who, playing tricks with conscience, dare not look at their own vices.*
—S.T. Coleridge, *Fears in Solitude*

William James, the eminent nineteenth-century scientist and philosopher, once remarked that "the purpose of an education is to know a good man when we see one." I recalled his observation last week while watching Lt. Col. Oliver North testify before the joint congressional hearings on the Iran-Contra affair.

After Friday afternoon's testimony, I went to see the Orioles play the Minnesota Twins. I still had James' observation in the back of my mind as I watched two men, perhaps in their twenties, parade a home-made banner through the crowd. The spray-painted sheet announced the formation of an Oliver North fan club. The banner received a standing ovation in every section. From aisle to aisle the fatigue-clad men proudly moved, and with them a kind of patriotic wave-cheer was created amidst the stifling summer heat.

Over the weekend, presidential spokesman Marlin Fitzwater reported that the White House had received 5,000 phone calls about the hearings, and all but twenty were salutary to Col. North. But still, I am reminded of the quote from William James: The purpose of an education is to know a good man when we see one.

Of course, courageous men are not always good men. Courage is a virtue only in so far as it is directed by prudence. The man sitting before the joint congressional committee last week is clearly a courageous man. On his chest, he wears a Silver Star, a Bronze Star, and two Purple Hearts, which attest to his acts of bravery.

But this courageous man has admitted he lied to Congress, to his superiors, to his business associates, to the Iranians, and to the Justice Department. He has admitted to destroying or falsifying documents, even after the investigation of his activities had begun. On Friday, he admitted to forming with former CIA head William Casey a kind of super-CIA, accountable to no one. The philosophical foundations for these lies and deception was a kind of frightening pragmatism—a dictum that states, not just that the end justified the means, but that a noble end, or what one believes to be a noble end, can be justified by any means, even if it circumvents the expressed intentions of Congress. Ironically, what Col. North believes to be a noble end, military aid to the contras, was still rejected by over half the Americans interviewed in a CBS news poll on Sunday. Just two days after Col. North's testimony, only thirty-three percent of those interviewed said they supported military aid to the contras.

Col. North's popularity may tell us more about our national character than we are willing to admit. These days, we tend to identify heroism with just courage, without understanding that real heroes possess moral character, something as indispensable to heroism as bravery, and something far more rare. Sisela Bok, in her book *On Lying*, points out that the regular telling of falsehoods silently erodes the character, until it is gradually but irrevocably changed like ancient stone statuary in public parks.

There is one man at the hearings who could give us all a lesson in what it means to be heroic. Senator Daniel Inouye, the chairman of the joint committees, swore in Col. North on Monday. Mr. Inouye did it with his left hand. His right arm was severed from his body during combat in World War II. After receiving a Distinguished

Service Cross and a Medal of Honor nomination, Senator Inouye began a career in public service marked by his integrity and courage. It must have been a little difficult for Senator Inouye when he listened to Col. North describe Congress as vacillating and fickle in regard to aid to the contras. It must have been doubly difficult for the senator when Col. North implied it was because Congress lacked the requisite courage to get the job done.

Samuel Johnson once made the observation that "Courage is a quality so necessary for maintaining virtue that it is always respected—even when it is associated with vice." I think Samuel Johnson probably knew a good man when he saw one.

*July, 1987*

# Meditations on the Nuclear Age

The word "prophet" is not used very much these days—at least not with that spelling. I thought quite a bit about the absence of the term from our national vocabulary while reading Philip Berrigan and Elizabeth McAlister's book, *The Time's Discipline* (an allusion to a poem by Wendell Berry on nuclear annihilation).

Something has happened to the concept of prophecy in the West. If it has not altogether died, it is certainly deeply comatose. What passes as prophecy these days is brought to us by television evangelists, long on snake oil and short on exegesis. These prophets for profit predict a dismal future here, and in the life beyond, for all those who don't get right with the Lord by anteing up to operators standing by at their toll-free numbers.

*The Time's Discipline* is a frightening book in many ways, probably because we don't recognize prophecy when we see it anymore. In the Old Testament, the words the Hebrew prophets offered were not their own, but those of God. Indeed, the Hebrew expression for prophecy in Jeremiah, Isaiah and Ezekiel is "the hand of God," as if these holy men were literally pulled along by the divine.

In Hebrew scripture prophets rarely told the future. They chastised, they exhorted, they sometimes overstated their case, reason frequently giving way to hyperbole, but always with a vision and a purpose: to reshape the nation of Israel as a nation of God.

The voice, or voices, in *Discipline* are prophetic in the Old Testament sense of the word. The book is a long meditation on the beatitudes, but it is also more specifically a meditation in several parts on the role of the prophet in a world that so often seems intent on committing suicide.

The very best sections of the book, and there are many, might be seen as a commentary on Longfellow's "My Lost Youth":

> The song and the silence in the heart
> That in part are prophecies and in part
> are longings wild and vain.

*The Time's Discipline* is a series of songs from the hearts of Berrigan and McAlister. But most of the love expressed in this book is *Agape,* not *Eros.* After reading *The Time's Discipline,* one is left wondering about the love they share for each other, a love that presumably had much to do with their both leaving the religious life. One of the most moving sections of the book is McAlister's tender confession about the longing for her children in the midst of one of her early imprisonments for "civil disobedience," a phrase they wish to replace with "acts of witness."

But the book is also, like Longfellow's prophet, sometimes wild. There is a similarity drawn between the American court system and Nazi jurisprudence; they also charge that in 1980 the FBI arranged the rape of a fellow protester to dissuade Berrigan, McAlister and others from a year of actions at the Pentagon. There is occasional special pleading and paraphrasing of biblical texts where there might have been more sober interpretation.

The book tells us much about organized nuclear resistance in this country, about what some might consider a "wild longing" for a world incapable of killing itself. Berrigan and McAlister have appended to their sometimes rambling meditation what they call "The Chronicle of Hope," a capsule history of actions taken by those affiliated with their community, Jonah House, over the last fifteen years. Often, as the authors point out, these actions were met with anger and physical and mental abuse.

These days, Berrigan and McAlister admit their longings are seen by many as wild. Only the verdict of history will tell us, or those who might discover what is left of us, if those longings were also in vain.

For now, although they do not mention the verse, they are perhaps comforted by Mark's gospel, Chapter 6, verse 4:

> *A prophet is not without honor except in his native place and among his own kin and in his own house.*

*April, 1989*

# See No Evil

On April 19th of this year six black and Hispanic youths raped and savagely beat a white female jogger in Central Park. In the month since the appalling incident, I have read or listened to over two dozen "explanations." One commentator, a faculty member at the Johns Hopkins University, suggested the brutal events were "indicative of a middle-class attitude of omnipotence." William Pfaff, a syndicated columnist, laid the blame on the "unhappy and unpalatable fact that racial tensions are growing in this country." A New York District Attorney, Elizabeth Holtzman, pointed out that "explanations which rely on race or class alone miss the key role that gender played in the incident."

This morning one of the television preachers served up another explanation: The devil was acting in the six young men. A common thread in these ostensible solutions to the mystery of evil is that the woman, the innocent sufferer, had done something wrong. It was her feeling of omnipotence; it was her foolishness in jogging in the park at night; it was the mistake of being female or white.

The commentaries remind me of Job's comforters. After the tragic Old Testament figure has lost his children, his house, his livestock and his farmland, three friends happen along to comfort him. Job is told by them that the reason he has suffered these extraordinary evils is that he has done something wrong. But the omniscient narrator of the tale very carefully points out in the opening line of the book that Job is blameless and upright, and thus we know the comforters, turned accusers, are mistaken.

Retributive justice—the notion that only the wicked are visited with evil, while the good remain unscathed—was a very popular point of view when the book of Job was written. The comforters were like the first pop social scientists. Their explanations for Job's suffering were offered before the winds that mysteriously leveled Job's home had abated.

In the early 1960s, Archibald MacLeish rewrote the book of Job in dramatic form. He called his play *J.B.* One of the most significant differences between the original work and MacLeish's version is that the comforters in *J.B.* are given different roles. One friend, Eliphaz, plays the part of a psychoanalyst. Another comforter, Zophar, is a cigar-smoking Marxist sociologist. Bildad, the third friend, is a born-again preacher. What the three comforters share with their ancient counterparts is their unwillingness to take Job/J.B.'s suffering seriously.

William James once remarked that the purpose of an education is to know a good man when we see one. I think he is probably right. But another element, one that seems to have been lost in the second half of this country of unparalleled evil, is knowing a bad person when we see one.

James saw it coming. At the turn of the century he remarked, "I can't seem to bring myself, as so many men are able to do, to blink evil out of sight, and gloss it over. It's as real as the good, and if it's denied, good must be denied too. It must be accepted and hated and resisted while there's breath in our bodies."

When we try to implicate the innocent, to accuse the sufferer of somehow bringing about her own misfortune, it is not really an attempt to lay blame. It is rather, I think, a vain effort at domesticating the terrible. After the time of Rousseau and eighteenth-century Optimism, we have succumbed to the notion that human beings are basically good. When we do evil, most social scientists tell us, it is because of a bad environment. But it is a curious fact that no one ever asks what kind of childhood Mother Teresa of Calcutta must have had.

We all know about those evil thoughts that pass through each of our minds. But we are no more responsible for these fleeting thoughts than a scarecrow is for the blackbirds that circle the crops he must guard. The responsibility in each case is to refuse to let them settle.

Why not say that on April 19th those evil thoughts found a home in the hearts and souls of six dangerous young men in Central Park? This explanation does nothing to demean the innocent sufferer. And it puts a terrible face back on the terrible.

*May, 1989*

# Klaus Barbie

*The past is not a package one can lay away.*
—Emily Dickinson

Last week the trial of Klaus Barbie, the former Gestapo chief known as "the butcher of Lyon," began in France. Barbie is accused of "crimes against humanity." The charges stem from his activities in the 1940s involving the deportation or execution of 11,000 French Jews, Gypsies and members of the resistance movement.

Barbie appeared in public last week for the first time since discovery and extradition from Bolivia in 1983. Testimony at his trial is expected to reveal that Barbie acted as a U.S. counter-intelligence agent in Germany immediately following World War II. A former American intelligence official, Erhard Dabringhaus, has indicated in several published reports that he employed Barbie to infiltrate German-speaking communist groups from 1948 to 1950. In return for intelligence information, Barbie was given money and protection from French attempts to extradite him. The French courts, on two separate occasions in the 1950s, had sentenced Barbie to death *in absentia.* For the thirty-two years before his arrest in 1983, he had lived in Bolivia as a businessman.

At the opening of his trial Barbie was angered by the amount and tenacity of the news coverage. His attorney, Jacques Verges, informed the 700 members of the media assembled for a press conference that "Mr. Barbie is outraged by the campaign of hypermedia publicity surrounding the trial." Barbie also suggested the special classes about the Holocaust given this month in French schools are unnecessary and inflammatory.

These comments came a few moments before a clerk began to read six hours worth of charges outlining acts of brutality and cruelty Barbie is said to have dealt his victims.

A few days into the trial, Barbie declared he was "a hostage and not a prisoner." He said he had been taken illegally from his Bolivian home. Barbie also announced he would no longer take part in his defense. He will spend the remainder of the trial back in St. Joseph's prison where he has been held for the past four years. Conscience and courage seem not to be suitable companions in the unfathomable psyche of Klaus Barbie. His accusers, victims of torture and deprivation, as well as family members of the dead, will be unable to confront Barbie face to face. James Baldwin reminds us, "It is in the face of one's victim, one sees oneself."

Barbie's indignation comes at a time when many people in Europe and America seem to be asking why we should remain preoccupied with the atrocities committed by the Nazis. These people ask why we should not forget about the past and move on.

There are many ways to begin to answer these questions. Most of the responses get caught in the throat. They sit there for just a moment until reason catches up with passion. It is important to separate, as best we can, justice from revenge. Without that distinction, it is too easy to become torturers ourselves.

One reason we must not forget the past is that the past, in a real sense, is the only time from which we may learn. The present is a succession of eye-blinks, fleeting instances destroyed in their birth. It is difficult to capture the truth in the present. The future is just as elusive, for it remains unseen. It is a pervasive darkness in which the human race as a whole is whistling.

In Western culture our metaphors for the past and future are surely misleading. The past is, in fact, in front of us. It can be seen quite clearly. The future is behind, as yet unobserved, as elusive as tomorrow's lottery number.

The past, though difficult to interpret, remains still, like a collection of images trapped in brittle photographs. We can hold them in our hands. We can examine them closely, hoping the contours come into focus. The past should not be something that paralyzes our possibilities in the present. It must be something that teaches us about the future, or how to avoid certain kinds of futures.

In a lecture given last Fall by Dr. Philip Hallie, a professor of philosophy at Wesleyan University, I was given one of the photographs that must never be forgotten. It came in the form of a story told to the professor by a guard at the Belzec concentration camp. A young French woman and her three-year-old daughter stood in line outside the gas chamber. As they moved into the dimly lit chamber, the little girl began to weep. She squeezed her mother's hand and said, "Mother, it's dark in here. It's so dark. And I have been so good."

*May, 1987*

# Thoughts on the Death of Bruno Bettleheim

> *I am killing myself to prove my independence and my new terrible freedom.*
> —Kirillov in Feodor Dostoevsky's *The Possessed*

> *Sometimes suicide is man's attempt to give final human meaning to a life that has become humanly meaningless.*
> —Dietrich Bonhoeffer, *Ethics*

"There is only one philosophical problem that is really serious, and that is suicide," opens Albert Camus in his essay, "Le Mythe de Sisyphe": "to decide whether life is worth living or not is to answer the fundamental question of philosophy."

Sometime last week, Bruno Bettleheim, octogenarian child psychologist and for eighteen months a resident of that living nightmare that was the Nazi death camps, decided to answer this most fundamental of questions in the negative.

In the days since his awesome decision many have wondered out loud how this humanitarian lover of children, protector of the most vulnerable among us, could take this final step of terrible freedom.

Reports in the newspapers mentioned his wife's death a few years ago and the more recent estrangement from his daughter. Others pointed out the grim reality that suicide rates in this country for elderly white males is dramatically higher than for any other group, three times that of white men twenty-five to thirty-five.

The morning I heard of Bettleheim's death I thought of the hours of enjoyment and uncommon insight I had found in his books. There was always a man who lay behind the books, a man with a sensitivity born of unspeakable evils powerful enough to have leveled so many others. There was a kindness in the books that only comes from those who know what it is like to try to survive where there is too little kindness.

In Woody Allen's recent film *Crimes and Misdemeanors,* the film maker introduces us to an alter-ego, a young documentary maker who befriends an old and wise philosopher, another victim/survivor of the death camps. The old man manages to convey a sense of life's importance, a meaning that goes beyond the surface detail of the Allen character's life.

The film maker decides to make a documentary about the philosopher, but in the midst of editing, the younger man learns the wise man has killed himself. All the old man leaves behind is an enigmatic note: "I have gone out the window."

In Bettleheim's death we can see an eerie kind of life imitating art. But judging by the commentaries, Bettleheim's suicide is seen by some as more a mystery than the leap of Allen's sage.

And yet, both found themselves alone at the end of lives that surely must, in those certain hours of the night, have seen their share of visitations from the spirits of the unsettled dead.

The message left by both these dead philosophers is that love ought to be enough, and that when life is broken, when it shatters into splinters that can only be seen clearly from the inside, then love alone is not nearly enough.

I have a friend, another octogenarian sage, a man with the numbers from Buchenwald tattooed on his arm. In an intimate moment many years ago he told me about the ghosts. They live in a territory he only half-remembers during the day and falls into at night.

My friend said that the survivors must every morning hear a strong and clear voice that tells them to get up, to live, to love. Some mornings the voice is only a whisper.

Last week, alone in a nursing home in Silver Spring, Bruno Bettleheim could not hear the voice at all.

*March, 1990*

# Furnace for Your Foe

*And can you impute a sinful deed
to babes who on their mothers' bosoms bleed?
Was there more vice in fallen Lisbon found,
than Paris where voluptuous joys abound?
Was there less debauchery to London known,
where opulence luxurious holds the throne?*
—Voltaire, *"Poeme sur le desastre de Lisbonne,"* 1755

*Repay evil with good, and lo, he between whom
and you there was enmity will become your warm friend.*
—The Koran, 625 A.D.

Shortly after 9:00 a.m. on All Saints Day, 1755, the earth heaved an enormous sigh and shrugged its massive shoulders in Lisbon, Portugal, leaving 50,000 people dead in the wake of an earthquake historians estimate at 8.0 on the Richter scale. In the first six minutes following the quake, thirty Catholic churches, containing some 15,000 people observing the holy day, were completely demolished.

One house, the residence of Sebastiano de Carvalho e Mello, the Marquis of Pombal, was left completely untouched. Senhor Carvalho e Mello, the ruling minister of the area was perhaps the most fervent anti-Jesuit in all Portugal.

A few days later, a Portuguese Jesuit, a Father Malagrida, explained that the quake and the tidal waves that followed a few days later were God's punishment for the sin proliferating in Lisbon.

Moslem leaders in North Africa and the Iberian Peninsula were quick to point out that the destruction had come as Allah's revenge upon the Portuguese Inquisition. This Islamic philosophical position seemed strong until after-shocks destroyed the mosque at al-Mansur in Rabat.

Meanwhile, Protestant leaders in London ascribed the disaster to divine retribution for Catholic crimes, both real and imagined. John Wesley, the founder of Methodism, preached a sermon on "The Cause and Cure of Earthquakes." "Sin," he reminded his followers, "is the moral cause of earthquakes, whatever their natural cause might be."

Wesley's sermon was on its way to the shores of New England when, on November 19, 1755, an earthquake damaged 1,500 Puritan homes in Boston.

Last Thursday, shortly after 12:30 a.m., the earth once again inexplicably shrugged its giant frame—and 50,000 people were left dead in cities called Rasht, Rudbar, and Kopeth on the Caspian Sea. The few survivors of Rudbar saw 95% of their city and surrounding farms destroyed in the first sixty seconds of the quake, which measured 7.7 on the Richter scale.

By Friday afternoon, like mid-eighteenth-century Europeans, our minds had turned to the metaphysics and politics of disaster. A commentator for National Public Radio offered that the quake might be seen as a good thing, for it could open lines of communication and sympathy for Iran. A few days later, *Time* asked whether "Iran's openness to aid signified a step toward *detente*..."

Closer to home, I overheard casual remarks from several people who opined that the earthquake was "deserved punishment" for the reign of the Ayatollah Khomeini—that it "couldn't have happened to nicer people."

I wondered if these offhand remarks were made by people who had seen any of the television reports from northern Iran: women in black chadors clinging to each other, wailing in black clusters of grief; stunned children wandering aimlessly amid the dead and injured; twisted arms and legs sticking out of rubble that two days before had been a house on fertile farm land, far from Tehran and the politics and metaphysics of hostages.

By Sunday afternoon, a team of French rescue workers with a score of search dogs had arrived to scenes of devastation. Japan had pledged $1.5 million in relief materials. England had sent its second plane full of medicine, clothing and other relief supplies, and the American Red Cross, as well as other private relief organization, had rushed in.

Back home, there were those of us in supermarket lines, at little league games, chatting over backyard fences and barbecues, who put order to the mystery by saying "what goes around comes around."

There is, of course, something dangerous about this theology of vindictiveness, which also makes a confident distinction between the innocent sufferers of AIDS (children, victims of contaminated blood transfusion), and the drug shooters and homosexuals who deserve it. But this kind of revenge is barren. It feeds on its own dreadful self. Indeed, if it is to a metaphysics of revenge we must look to discover an answer to the tragic mystery of the Iranian earthquake, we would also do well to heed the advice of Shakespeare's Norfolk in *Henry VIII:*

> *Heat not a furnace for your foe*
> *so hot*
> *that is does singe yourself.*

*July, 1990*

# Religion

*If we subject everything to reason, our religion will have nothing mysterious or supernatural: if we violate the principle of reason, our religion will be absurd and ridiculous*
—BLAISE PASCAL

# Religion in the 80s:
## *Mileposts, Murder, the Moral Majority, and Much, Much More*

NBC ended its December 31, 1989 evening news coverage with a montage of the most important stories of the 1980s. It was a collection of small bits of news bytes, those thirty-second wrestling matches between fact and oversimplification through which most of us learn about ourselves and the world.

There on the screen in a rapid succession of still pictures, with a synchronized drumbeat keeping pulse with the images, our lives passed before our eyes, ten years of life fit on the head of an electronic pin, a decade of experience compressed into a thimble-full of viewing. After the segment—sometime in the midst of watching a very small dog pull a miniature chuck wagon across the screen—it occurred to me that the decade-ending wrap-up was missing something important. In the entire three-minute montage not one image, except a two-second glance at the worried face of Jim Bakker, evoked the great religious stories of the 1980s.

In a decade that began with day fifty-nine of a hostage crisis directly attributed to the rise of Shiite Islam, and ended with General Manuel Noriega receiving temporary asylum in the papal nuncio's residence in Panama, it would be safe to say that religion, like an unwanted dinner guest to some, or a trusted companion to others, insinuated itself into countless aspects of our individual and collective everyday lives.

Religious scandals alone might have filled the three-minute montage. In 1982 the Vatican bank uncovered

$1.4 billion in questionable loans made by Archbishop Paul Marcinkus to Italy's largest private bank, the Banco Ambrosiano. A few weeks later, Ambrosiano's president, Roberto Calvi, was found hanging from Blackfriars Bridge in London.

In the same year, a federal grand jury investigation revealed that Cardinal John Cody of Chicago had diverted tax-exempt church funds to a life-long female friend. The probe ended when Cody died in April of 1982.

In 1983, the Reverend Sun Yung Moon, the Korean-born evangelist and founder of the Unification Church, was sentenced to eighteen months in prison for tax fraud and conspiracy to obstruct justice.

A short time later, a California court took away the tax-exempt status of the Crystal Cathedral, the $18 million home of Reverend Robert Schuller's television ministry in Garden Grove, California, and a middle-aged man who owns a packaging factory in the Bronx began to be worshipped as the "Cosmic Puppeteer" by a small religious sect in India.

The end of the 1980s brought the vision of a 900-foot Jesus to television preacher Oral Roberts, though there were no reports of others in the neighborhood seeing anyone that tall. A year later, in 1987, the Reverend Roberts warned his followers that if they did not help him raise several million dollars for his financially ailing hospital God would "call him home." 1988 saw the downfall of Jimmy Swaggart and Jim Bakker, two televangelists who might have been created by Flannery O'Connor.

A number of important religious mileposts were passed in the decade just ended. The 500th anniversary of the birth of Martin Luther was celebrated throughout Germany and Scandinavia. In Stockholm the celebration was used as an occasion for bringing old enmities to rest between Luther's followers and Jews offended by the sixteenth-century reformer's anti-Semitic remarks. The statement of the Lutheran delegation read in part: "We cannot accept nor condone the violent verbal attacks that the reformer made against the Jews."

The 1980s also saw the first visit by a pope to the synagogue in Rome; the first visit of a Soviet premier to the Vatican; the three branches of American Lutheranism voting to merge into one organization with 5.3 million members; the election of the first women bishops in the Methodist and Episcopal churches; and the first female admitted for rabbinical studies at the Jewish Theological Seminary in New York.

Perhaps the most significant mileposts of the decade were passed without any fanfare: In 1985, for the first time in 2,000 years of Christianity, there were more adherents to that faith in the southern hemisphere than in the northern. A year later, by most international population estimates, one out of every five people on earth was now a Moslem. In fact, today, Islam is the fastest growing of the world's religions.

Murder and martyrdom were all too frequently in the religious news of the 1980s. Three Maryknoll nuns and a lay woman were killed in El Salvador in December, 1980. In a grim closing of the parentheses, the lives of six Jesuit priests, their cook, and her fifteen-year-old daughter were taken in the same country toward the end of 1989. Between these two events stood too many violent religious punctuation marks: the murder of India's Prime Minister Indira Ghandi by Sikhs; the slaying of Father Jerzy Popieluszko, a popular supporter of the then-outlawed Solidarity labor movement, by agents of the Polish secret police; bloodshed in Tibet that erupted when Buddhist monks attempted to lead a peaceful demonstration calling for Tibetan independence from China; the threatening of the life of Salman Rushdie, author of *The Satanic Verses,* by the Ayatollah Khomeini who himself returned to Allah at the end of the decade past; and the bizarre case of Mark Hoffmann and the Mormon Salamander murders in 1987. Mr. Hoffmann, born and raised a Mormon, admitted forging a number of documents that seemed to call into question the accepted version of the Church of the Latter Day Saints' origins. He also confessed to two car bomb murders committed to prevent the forgeries from being revealed.

In other religious events of the 1980s, the Moral Majority, that precarious hybrid of religion and politics, was born, grew, and died; the Dali Lama and Bishop Desmond Tutu won Nobel peace prizes; American court cases were decided against public Christmas Nativity displays, creationism, and school prayer, and in favor of Greenville, Tennessee, parents who objected on religious grounds to their children reading Hans Christian Andersen, *The Diary of Anne Frank,* and a story in which a girl reads to a boy while he is cooking.

In the 1980s, the scientific works of Galileo Galilei, after 350 years, were finally removed from the Vatican's index of forbidden books, but the Catholic hierarchy was not nearly as kind to Father Charles Curran, Archbishop Raymond Hunthausen of Seattle, and Dominican priest Matthew Fox, all of whom received various forms of reprimand for straying too far from a 1980s Vatican that to some seemed long on dogma and short on forgiveness.

Rewards for the religious quotes of the decade must go to David Hubbard, Jerry Falwell, and Mikhail Gorbachev. Mr. Hubbard, commenting on the conservative and accusatory swing of the evangelical Christianity in the early part of the decade, wryly commented that "Evangelical Christianity threatens to become a spiritual version of the National Rifle Association."

The Reverend Falwell, after a five-day trip to South Africa in 1985, announced that "If Bishop Tutu maintains he speaks for the black people of South Africa, he is a phony."

And at the decade's end, Mikhail Gorbachev, after fifty years of unconscionable acts by the Soviet government against Jewish and Gentile believers alike, suggested for all the world to hear that "People of many confessions including Christians, Moslems, Jews, Buddhists, and others live in the Soviet Union. All of them have a right to satisfy their spiritual needs."

Any attempt at a coherent analysis of religious trends in the 1980s must surely meet with failure. One out of every three Americans at the beginning of the decade identified himself or herself as "born again," members of Congress and presidential candidates regularly wore their religion on their sleeves, yet church attendance was down for the entire 1980s. This was a decade where the Catholic Church used sophisticated carbon dating techniques to prove that the Shroud of Turin is a fake, while a special team of Talmudic scholars and technicians at Jerusalem's Institute for Science and Halacha cleverly turned out devices to operate electric lights and elevators without human intervention, so that devout but modern Jews might more easily observe the Sabbath.

The 1980s was a decade where American Catholic bishops wrote progressive and far-reaching documents on nuclear arms and economic issues, while taking no real stand against the Vatican's position on birth control, despite the fact that the hierarchy's point of view is largely ignored in America.

Some American Jewish groups that had long defended the State of Israel under almost any conditions developed sharp criticisms against the Israeli government after troops began beating young Palestinians suspected of taking part in a protest of Israel's occupation of the West Bank and Gaza.

While the Presbyterian Church was sharply divided over charges that the denomination's liberal leadership had forced some conservative congregations to violate biblical standards by insisting that every congregation must elect female elders, a feisty Donna Hanson, president of the Catholic National Lay Advisory Council, told Pope John Paul II in San Francisco: "Though I know the church is not a democracy ruled by popular vote, I expect to be treated as a mature, educated, and responsible adult."

The decade began with President Ronald Reagan declaring that the Soviet Union was an "evil empire." It ended with religious freedoms openly supported by the

Soviet premier. It has been a tough decade to figure. There probably has been no ten-year period as decisive for the world's religions. There may never be another like it.

It's a shame NBC missed it.

*January, 1990*

# The Vatican and Contraception

Joseph Wood Krutch in 1929 made a prophetic observation:

> Science has always promised two things not necessarily related—an increase first in our powers, second in our happiness or wisdom, and we have come to realize that it is the first and less important of the promises which it has kept most abundantly.

When the Vatican issued a 12,000-word report condemning a wide range of birth technologies, I thought of Krutch's remark. It might have served as an epigraph for the Vatican document, which offers negative evaluation of cloning, artificial insemination, human-animal hybrids, surrogate mothering and *in vitro* fertilization. The document warns against these technologies because "the uncontrolled application of such techniques could lead to unforeseeable and damaging consequences for civil society." The writers of the report are clearly concerned that science confers power, not purpose. Technology is only a blessing, they argue, if those purposes are ethically sound. Science has the ability to do a near-infinite number of things, but it cannot, by itself, discriminate what is worth doing.

The Vatican attempts to outline what is "worth doing." The document is a courageous attempt at dealing with a range of issues that have remained difficult and elusive to both ethicists and scientists.

Still, although the church deserves credit for wrestling with these complex issues, a forty-page document is probably not the place to attempt to solve them. Vastly different procreative technologies are lumped together in the report. The document condemns as "fundamentally sinful" any fertilization achieved outside the bodies of married couples. By reflexively placing *in vitro* fertilization together with other more morally questionable technologies, the writers have produced two great ironies.

The first can only be understood by knowing a little of the history of the church's position on artificial insemination and test-tube babies. In 1951 the Vatican first took official notice of *in vitro* fertilization. Pope Pius XII extended a condemnation he had issued two years earlier against artificial insemination. His comments on *in vitro* fertilization, like his earlier ban on artificial insemination, extended even to married couples who were using their own sperm and ova for the fertilization. In 1956, Pius repeated the condemnation in a tough speech presented at the World Congress on Fertility and Sterility.

In objecting to the idea of *in vitro* fertilization, Pius used the same two lines of reasoning; first, that semen used in the process of *in vitro* fertilization would have to be obtained by masturbation, a practice with a long history of moral recrimination attached to it. The second was the notion that *in vitro* fertilization, if perfected, would disrupt the natural relationship between loving couples. The fertilization, the pope argued, would not be the product of "sacred conjugal union."

The first great irony of the current Vatican document is that its shapers failed to see that *in vitro* fertilization resorts to masturbation, but for precisely the opposite reasons the church has condemned it as "self-abuse." *In vitro* fertilization uses masturbation as part of a process that produces children.

Vincent McNabb in his contemplative work *From a Friar's Cell,* once wrote, "Nowhere more than in ecclesiastical politics and doctrine do words prove themselves the veils of thought." If a less pejorative term were used to describe the gathering of semen, I wonder if the church might have found it morally acceptable. Language, as

T.S. Eliot reminds us, has a way of shaping if not producing reality. It is as if the word *masturbation* has taken on the character of the intrinsically evil, when in fact earlier pronouncements of the church suggest it is morally wrong only because it does not produce children.

The church's latest pronouncement moves quickly but very quietly from the factual claim that in the past masturbation has involved "self-defilement" to the rather dubious moral claim that it must always be that way.

The second irony involves Pius' other argument against *in vitro* fertilization. The language of all of the mid-century pontiff's remarks on procreative technologies is so similar to the latest Vatican missive that the irony extends there as well.

Pius warned against "turning the sanctuary of the family into nothing more than a biological laboratory." The 1987 report suggests *in vitro* fertilization "establishes the dominion of technology over the origin and destiny of the human person." Both Pius and the writers of the latest Vatican document suggest the children of *in vitro* fertilization are not the products of "sacred conjugal love."

But think. How many children born these days by the normal process of sexual intercourse are the products of "sacred conjugal love"? Heywood Broun reminds us: "The ability to make love frivolously is the chief characteristic which distinguishes human beings from beasts." Indeed, the church in the past has taught that in time of sickness, in the last stages of pregnancy, there is sometimes a greater love that goes beyond conjugal union, a love that transcends the physical. It may be that the parents of children conceived through *in vitro* fertilization are expressing just that kind of love.

Perhaps the supreme irony in the modern church's position on non-conjugal procreation is that Pius made one of his forceful attacks on December 24, 1953. The next day, of course, we celebrated the result of one of humankind's most celebrated non-conjugal unions.

*November, 1988*

# Religion and Hats

Have you ever noticed that the world's great religious traditions all have terrific hats? I have been thinking about this for some time. The realization did not come all at once. It developed in a kind of cumulative effect. A papal crown here, a yarmulke there; it all added up.

I began to understand the important role hats play in religious circles when I was a small child in Catholic grade school. The 1950s were a time when sin was still sin, and people were sent to hell for murder, robbing banks, and eating meat on Friday. This was a time in the church when it was easy to figure out who the most important men were in the Catholic Church. They were allowed to wear their hats in church.

At a high mass, altar boys, priests, monsignors, and sometimes even bishops would line up, serene looks on their faces and great hats on their heads.

Ordinarily priests wore something called a beretta, a black hat about the size and shape of a giant Jujy Fruit. The monsignors topped their berettas off with purple pompoms. The bishops got to wear two hats at once: a little beanie underneath, called a zucchetto, and a mitre on the top, an impressive looking piece of headgear that looked like a miniature Gothic Cathedral sitting on the bishop's head.

Although the most important men in the Roman Catholic tradition got to wear their hats in church, all the women and girls were required, under the sartorial sins section of canon law, to cover their heads while worshipping.

In the first through fifth grades of my elementary school the girls wore little blue beanies that matched their navy and white starched uniforms. In the sixth grade the girls were permitted to see a health film the boys didn't get to watch. The girls began to act differently. They also turned in their blue beanies for something called a chapel veil, a shear black lace affair that looked very much like what Rita Moreno must have worn to the funeral parlor after her boyfriend was stabbed in *West Side Story*.

Sometimes my sisters or their friends would forget their chapel veils and thus secure to the tops of their forgetful heads pieces of kleenex, each anchored by a half-dozen strategically placed bobby-pins. All Catholic girls in the sixth grade seemed to have an inexhaustible supply of bobby-pins. It may have had something to do with the health film the boys did not get to watch. I don't know.

Right in the middle of the eight o'clock mass I would look up from the consecration to discover a variety of my classmates with pieces of kleenex attached to their heads so as not to offend the Almighty. I wondered what God must have thought looking down from his infinite height at a small sea of blue-beanied and chapel-veiled schoolgirls, with a kleenex-topped sixth grader here and there.

But it was in these moments of theological reflection I began to understand the importance of proper headgear in religious devotion. Since that time, I have made a small but impressive study of the role hats play in various religious traditions.

The Tibetan monks wear an interesting looking stocking cap with earflaps, a kind of mystical aviator's headgear. The patriarch of the Russian Orthodox Church, a man who has been getting quite a bit of media time in this era of glasnost, has been showing off a variety of interesting hats that range from a simple white pill box model with matching veil, to a jeweled crown that looks very much like the hat worn by the infant of Prague, a small but impressively dressed doll that made the rounds of enthusiastic Catholic homes in the 1950s. The infant of Prague came in his own little box, and was decked out in white and purple robes and a great hat. He looked like a beatific cousin of Barbie and Ken.

The Cantor's hat in the Jewish tradition is an impressive piece of head wear. It looks very much like something a Japanese sushi chef might wear. The Muslim Sufis have some great hats, not to mention the Japanese Shintos, and Mahayana Buddhist holy men. Although we may not like the politics of the Ayatollah Khomeini, he still has good hats. And there is impressive headgear to be found in classical Hinduism, Greek Orthodoxy, among the Sikhs in India, and in various African religious traditions.

All of these observations bring me quite naturally to the Reverend Sun Yung and the Reverend Jimmy Swaggart. There has been some debate lately about their worthiness as religious leaders. After some thoughtful analysis, as well as some serious theological reflection, I would like to suggest that neither man is capable of leading a great world-wide religious movement. My decision has little to do with their moral characters, or even with their theology. They just don't have good hats.

*July, 1988*

# How to Play Both Sides of Creation Street

When the Supreme Court late last month struck down a Louisiana law that required the teaching of creationism whenever evolution is taught in the public schools, Wendell Bird, the Atlanta lawyer for the creationists, called it a victory for his side.

Bird referred to a passage in the opinion suggesting that

> teaching a variety of scientific theories about the origins of humankind to school children might be validly done with the clear secular intent of enhancing the effectiveness of science instruction.

But Bird's interpretation represents a curious shifting of ground that goes on among the creationists with respect to the classification of their beliefs as religious or scientific.

In the past few years, in a number of court cases in California, Louisiana and Arkansas, the creationists have argued that their beliefs do in fact constitute a religious point of view. But they have also contended that textbooks which contain evolutionary theory teach a "'religion of secular humanism," and thus should be banned as well.

After the latest Supreme Court ruling, Bird suggested that the creationists' view is not a religious one, and should be examined solely on its scientific merits. This problem of identity, or this tactic of labeling creationist ideas as religious or scientific, depending on the situation, has existed at least since the publication of Henry Morris' *Scientific Creationism* in 1974. Morris' Institute for Creation Research publishes two editions of his book, one which argues, with the aid of biblical references, that creationism is a religious point of view, and the other, the "public school edition," without accompanying biblical references, which suggests its claims should be taken as scientific ones.

In all this subterfuge a clear view of the nature of "science" and its distinction from "religion" somehow gets lost. There is a subtle logic here that is worthy of the Red King in *Alice in Wonderland,* who suggests the beheading of the headless.

A second observation about the creationists' current efforts is directly related to the first. Suppose we grant the claim that the creationists are in fact making scientific observations about the nature and origin of the universe, and further, that they deserve equal time with evolutionary theory in the biology curriculum of public schools. Why should we only grant equal time to Jews and Christians who happen to share the same creation story?

The Indian *Book of Manu* suggests that the universe was once a chaotic darkness. God, the great creator of all things, drove away the darkness by his light, creating the great seas in the process. In the midst of the waters the god placed a seed. Out of the seed developed a golden egg in which the god Brahma sat for a whole year in calm meditation. Finally, he broke the egg, the two halves forming the heavens and the earth.

The Zoroastrians believe Ahura Mazda created the heavens and the earth, determined the paths of the stars, caused the moon to wax and wane and created the two great spirits, Ahriman, absolute goodness, and the evil Angra Mainya.

In the Siamese tradition of fourth-century China, P'an Ku chiseled the universe out of chaos. After his work was complete, he benevolently changed his bones to rocks, his flesh to earth, marrow, teeth and nails to metals, breath to wind, veins to rivers, and his four limbs to the pillars which mark the boundaries of the universe.

The Koran suggests that Allah created the world in six days, but a tradition in the Muslim Sahih says that Allah created the earth on Saturday, mountains on Sunday, trees on Monday, objectionable things on Tuesday, light on Wednesday, animals on Thursday and Adam late Friday afternoon.

Not all schools of Buddhism have a concern with cosmogony (from the Greek *cosmos* and *genesis*). But among the three schools where there is an interest in the concept of creation all agree that there are an infinite number of worlds, each lasting 4,320,000 years.

All of these points of view, of course, are in direct conflict with the biblical account of creation. They are also in contradiction to Jainist doctrines of the cosmos. For the devout Jain, the universe, which is composed of living and material substances, is in constant flux, though it has no beginning and no end. This point of view is actually expressed in a number of different tales in the Jain tradition. Indeed, the particulars of those tales often contradict one another. Hinduism, Buddhism, Taoism and Confucianism also have several competing stories within their own traditions about the origin of the universe. A few years ago, Morris, the founder of the Institute for Creation Research, suggested we should "present as many theories as possible and give the child the right to choose the one that seems most logical to him." I wonder if Morris really has any idea how many competing creation myths there are in the religious background of Americans. To prefer one of these stories over the others, without thorough analysis, would appear to be quite unscientific.

This point about the variety of creation accounts leads quite naturally to a third observation. If one looks very carefully at the first two chapters of Genesis, it becomes clear that there are actually two accounts of creation to be found there. Genesis 1:1 to 2:3 is a highly structured, repetitious, semipoetic account of creation by a god named Elohim. This is followed, however, by an account in Genesis 2:4 to 2:25, where the order of events is different from chapter one, the style is much more prosaic, and the deity is called Yahweh.

Chapter one begins with a progression of creation culminating in verse 25 with Elohim making man in his image and likeness on the sixth day. Chapter two suggests that "in the same day Yahweh made the earth and the heavens" (day two in chapter one), he formed man from dust. One of the major problems with teaching the biblical account of creation as a scientific theory is deciding which of the differing accounts we wish to give scientific status.

The final observation to be made about the creationist has to do with possible causes, as opposed to the manifestation, of the widespread belief that creationism is a viable scientific point of view. The government-sponsored National Assessment of Educational Progress, in its most recent survey of science knowledge in the nation found that few seventeen-year-olds can describe the scientific method. Only thirty-nine percent of the young adults can respond correctly to simple questions about evolutionary theory. A quarter of the adults think humans have been on earth less than 100,000 years. How much of this ignorance is related to the popularity of creationist ideas?

Moreover, this fuzziness is not confined to the young. A successful presidential candidate had this to say about evolution shortly before the 1980 election:

> Well, it is a theory, it is a scientific theory only, and it has in recent years been challenged in the world of science and not yet believed in the scientific community to be infallible as it once was believed. But if it was going to be taught in the schools, then I think that also the biblical theory of creation, which is not a theory but the biblical story of creation should also be taught.

The Red King would have been proud.

*July, 1987*

# Know Them by Their Fingernails

Last week the Reverend Jimmy Swaggart announced from his Baton Rouge headquarters that he will defy the Assemblies of God order that he step down from the pulpit for a full year. Swaggart stopped preaching on February 21 after a tearful confession that he had sinned with a prostitute. In last week's announcement, Swaggart said he would return to the pulpit May 22, just three months after the disclosure of his moral indiscretion.

The day following Swaggart's latest announcement, the Reverend Mike Evans, pastor of the Church on the Move in Euless, Texas, shed some light on his fellow minister's rather accelerated spiritual recovery.

Evans disclosed that the Reverend Oral Roberts, the Tulsa-based television evangelist, had called Swaggart to say he had seen demons with long fingernails digging into the skin of the Louisiana preacher. Roberts assured Swaggart that he had effectively cast out the demons, cuticles and all. Evans offered the opinion that Swaggart's recent feeling of being "released from sin" might be related to the exorcism by Roberts. Evans added that the casting out by Roberts explained "some of the rationale behind Reverend Swaggart's decision to return to television after three months' suspension."

This newest revelation by Swaggart comes as one in a long series of communications with the supernatural, including the warning to Roberts last spring that he would be "called home" if he failed to raise $2 million for his ailing hospital. The hospital had been built on the campus of the Oral Roberts University after Roberts received a revelation from a 900-foot Jesus.

Since last week's announcement, I have been wondering if Roberts might take a good look at Attorney General, Edwin Meese III, to see if he could detect the telltale long fingernails sticking out of the counselor's scalp. It might be of some real assistance to the Department of Justice. It also might explain where the demons went after Roberts evicted them from Swaggart; but this only explains the whereabouts of some of the demons with the long fingernails; we know, of course, they travel in legion.

For the record—and on the off-chance someone in real authority may read this—I'd like to suggest that the remainder of the demons are now employed as manicurists in a prominent unisex hair salon in Baltimore. I know this if hard to believe, but all the evidence points to the fact that the same fingernails that just a few weeks ago were dug into the flesh of Swaggart are now cutting the cuticles and French manicuring the fingertips of unsuspecting women all over the city.

The first bit of evidence came when I discovered, the very same day Roberts drove out the demons, the mysterious hiring of three new manicurists at a certain unisex hair salon. Mere coincidence? I think not.

On the very same day Swaggart's demons were cast out and this certain unisex hair salon hired the three new manicurists, the salon began a spring manicure special for $6.66.

I have since discovered through means I am not at liberty to disclose that if you play in reverse the Muzak of this certain unisex hair salon, what appears to be the Ray Coniff Singers doing "Born Free" is, in reality, a Satanic message revealing that Madge of the Palmolive liquid television commercials is really Beelzebub. She has been sending her minions out to sink their long fingernails into the skin of unsuspecting television preachers, the attorney general, and various other individuals in state and local government, as well as in the private sector.

No longer can any of us consider ourselves safe. Just this morning I attached two emery boards in the form of a cross to my front door. I would suggest you do the same. In the meantime, we all would do well to keep in mind the words of the Reverend Oral Roberts: "By their fingernails shall ye know them."

*April, 1988*

# Giving Christ a Bad Name

> *If you are going to call yourself a Christian,
> don't let Christ get a bad name on your account.*
> —Cyril of Jerusalem,
> *Catechetical Lectures,* 350 A.D.

In the past few years "Christian" has become a bad word, one that causes many people I respect to make faces when it is used in their presence. Their attitude began to develop, I suspect, a few years ago when presidential candidates began to wear their Christianity on their sleeves. Reporters in the 1980 and 1984 campaigns regularly asked both Republicans and Democrats if they were Christians. The question was posed, and usually answered, as if interrogators and candidates all had some univocal understanding of what the word meant.

My friends' discomfort with the word "Christian" became more pronounced in the mid-1980s when the word somehow became co-opted by a group of people who proudly wrapped the Christian tradition in a kind of rigidity and literalism that is hard for most sensitive and intelligent people to embrace. It is something akin to the political patent the Republicans seem to have taken possession of with respect to words like "American" and "patriotism." At about the same time, my friends pointed out that the word "Christian" was the term chosen by a collection of flim-flam artists who make Elmer Gantry look like Saint Francis of Assissi.

The Reverend Jim Bakker's infidelity and subsequent blackmail, the Reverend Sun Yung Moon's difficulties with the Internal Revenue Service, Oral Roberts' latest exercise in human extortion for reportedly divine purposes, and the Reverend Jimmy Swaggart's admission of improper sexual conduct, all serve as painful reminders of just how far the word "Christian" has fallen in the 2,000 years of its use. These revelations have done much to reinforce my friends' already uncomplimentary view of what a Christian is and does.

Karl Barth, the great twentieth-century Protestant theologian, reminds us that "faith is never identical with piety." What has made my friends snicker just a bit about Bakker and Swaggart is that the pair frequently preached about a god who was long on judgment and short on forgiveness. For both men, faith and public piety became synonymous. In a real way, Bakker and Swaggart spent so much time telling us that we should be punished for our sins that the media saw to it that they were punished *by* theirs. It is a rare person, as Montaigne reminds us, who can rid himself of what he condemns.

Still, I am not entirely comfortable with the reaction of my friends. One can admit that they are correct about Swaggart and Bakker. There is nothing more unattractive and illogical than aggressive Christianity. One can also concur that it does a disservice to the truth when virtues like compassion and kindness are referred to as peculiarly Christian attributes. One wonders what these conservative Christians think devout Hindus and Buddhists were doing centuries before the time of Christ.

Andre Gide once remarked that he would not be surprised if Christianity were found at the bottom of Pandora's box. I have heard many of my friends applaud Gide's observation, as well as a comment made by G.B. Shaw: "Christianity might be a good thing if anyone ever tried it."

We sometimes forget—Jesus did.

*November, 1987*

# An Irony at the Vatican

*A system of dogmas may be the ark within which the Church floats safely down the flood-tide of history. But the Church will perish unless it opens the window and lets out the dove to search for an olive branch.*
—Alfred North Whitehead,
*Religion in the Making,* 1926

The presidents of several American Catholic colleges and universities returned recently from a Vatican meeting called to discuss the relationship of Catholic institutions of higher education to the church hierarchy.

Last year, Vatican officials outlined a number of proposed rules that would give church authorities control over Catholic colleges and universities world-wide, including a requirement that all theology teachers have papal permission before they teach.

The American presidents met along with 175 representatives from Catholic institutions of higher education about the world to discuss the first draft of a 7,000-word document proposed last summer by the Vatican Congregation for Catholic Education.

Last year's draft called for schools to "maintain strict and faithful relations" with local bishops to ensure "the principles of Catholic doctrine are faithfully observed." Another section of the first draft urges that teachers must be distinguished not only by competence but by "doctrinal integrity and uprightness of life. Those who lack these requirements are to be dismissed."

Further provisions of the document explicitly require that anyone teaching theology at Catholic colleges must have a "mandate from competent ecclesiastical authority."

Reactions from the American presidents attending the recent meeting have been cautious, while at the same time clear and well-argued. They suggest, among other things, that the Congregation for Catholic Education's proposed rules could have disastrous consequences, for the document would not only limit academic freedom, but would also put a virtual end to federal funding of Catholic institutions. For these and other reasons, most of the 175 delegates urged a revamping of the document.

Although these are surely compelling reasons for rewriting the document, one major irony in this story has, as yet, gone unnoticed. In order to understand this irony we must return to 1274, the year of Thomas Aquinas, the Angelic Doctor's death.

In his lifetime, the great Italian thinker had not secured total victory for his blending of Aristotle and Church teaching. Less than three years after his death, at the prompting of Pope John XXI, the bishop of Paris issued a decree banning 219 of Thomas Aquinas' theological propositions as heretical.

A few weeks after the Paris decree, Robert Kolwardby, a fellow Dominican friar of Thomas', persuaded officials at Oxford to ban various of the Italian theologian's doctrines. A short time later, a Franciscan, William de la Mare in his *Correctorium Fratis Thomae,* suggested Thomas was to be branded a heretic on 118 issues. This work prompted John Peckham, a Franciscan and Archbishop of Canterbury, to officially condemn Thomas Aquinas as a "dangerous theological thinker."

Over the next fifty years, the French and German Dominicans mounted a campaign to rehabilitate the name of Thomas Aquinas. After some expert theological and political maneuvering they convinced Pope John XXII, no friend of the Franciscans, to press for the canonization of Thomas Aquinas as a saint. In 1323, ninety-eight years after his birth and forty-six years after his original condemnation, the Angelic Doctor was elevated to sainthood in the Catholic Church.

Two centuries later, at the Council of Trent (1545-1563), Thomas' *Summa Theologica* was placed on the altar alongside the Bible. By 1879, Pope Leo XIII, in his encyclical *On the Restoration of Christian Philosophy,* confirmed the "pre-eminence and special status of Thomas among philosophers of the Church." This position was reaffirmed in 1921 by Pope Benedict XV, who directed that the education of all priests in philosophy and theology was to be done primarily with the writings of Thomas Aquinas.

The irony, of course, should now be quite clear. A central element to any Vatican doctrinal litmus test of contemporary teachers of philosophy and theology must include the writings of Thomas Aquinas. But had a similar document already been passed in 1277, we would have never heard of the Angelic Doctor. It was only through the philosophical and theological debate provided in the context of the university that Thomas Aquinas was eventually given the hearing he deserved.

The story of Thomas Aquinas provides a helpful reminder of the difference between the functions of the university and that of the Church. Moreover, if the Vatican Congregation for Catholic Education were to ignore the recommendations of the 175 member delegation and pass last year's document without amending, we would have no way of knowing what other future angelic doctors there might have been.

*May, 1989*

# The Infinite Became Finite in a Tiny Child

There is something about the passage of time that changes when you find out there is no Santa Claus. Time before then had seemed immeasurably long—particularly the interval between Thanksgiving and Christmas. It was, perhaps, a subtle way of finding room for boundless hope.

After the revelation came that morning in the yard behind Johnny Hucke's house, the concept of time and the nature of hope at once began a process of inexorable transformation. In the middle of "King of the Hill," Johnny had paused, a look of age spreading over his ten-year-old face. "You know," he said seriously, "there is no Santa Claus." This was quickly followed by the marshaling of evidence. Myriad facts about the nature of reindeer, the life expectancy of elves, and the size and shape of the average American chimney were laid one atop the other until something enormous had been constructed that could not be walked around or climbed over.

I think I was eight years old at the time, by today's standards an embarrassingly late age to be losing such dreams. Sometimes we leave behind important, perhaps better, parts of ourselves. We treat these parts like a hurried and overburdened traveler might treat an offered bouquet of flowers. Early in our lives we begin to jettison those parts of ourselves that make travel to adulthood more difficult. They are often those things about us that are most easily subject to ridicule.

Those more naive hopes about Christmas were soon replaced by larger commercial ones. My life as a nine-

and ten-year old was largely governed during the holiday season by what I might expect from struggling parents who had replaced the jolly man in the red suit. I never stopped to think throughout the remainder of childhood and adolescence about their hopes, and about sacrifices they must have made to make each of their offspring feel like an only child on Christmas day.

Now, many years later, at Christmas, that more profound and thus naive sense of hope returns. For the past few years that time between Thanksgiving and Christmas again seems an eternity.

In this time, I begin to think about those better parts of myself—the ones I began to jettison at the age of eight. I am sure there was openness and vulnerability and a tenderness for people I didn't even know. These parts were left on a hill behind Johnny Hucke's house. They were discarded along with a larger notion of hope.

At Christmas time, for a few days at least, they mysteriously return. I walk around thinking about Arabs and Israelis coming to some lasting sort of peace. I think about a day when baby carriages will no longer explode in northern Ireland, and when South Africans of all colors will be proud of their country. In the past few holiday seasons I have mused about this fleeting sense of hope, the larger kind, and then I have thought about the impossibility of its permanence.

This year, as Christmas approaches, I am once again filled with a larger sense of hope, a longing for the better parts of myself. For Christians, this longing is tied to a deeper mystery, that in a strange little corner of the world, nearly 2,000 years ago, a child was born to a sweaty, unemployed carpenter and a frightened, teenage mother. And in that moment, the infinite became finite in that tiny child. God had devised a subtle way for humans to find room for boundless hope.

*December, 1988*

# Reading, Writing & Teaching

*A school teacher should have an atmosphere of awe, and walk wonderingly, as if he were amazed at being himself.*
—WALTER BAGEHOT

# Dancing with My Students

*Learn to dance, not so much for the dancing.*
—G.K. Chesterton

I have been reflecting this evening—just hours after closing my lecture notes for the seventeenth year of teaching—how true is George Eliot's observation that nothing is as good as it seems beforehand. I am wondering what this woman, forced to use a man's voice, was thinking when she wrote this line. I know very little of Eliot's life, but I am wondering if she might have been thinking of the expectation that comes with teaching.

On that first day, faces are fresh, stories are untold, possibilities hang in the air like vapors, each waiting to be called into the actual. But by the final day, even in the best of classes, there is a kind of sadness, a disappointment that lingers, at least on my side of the lectern. It is a dissatisfaction not so much with my students as with my inability to reach certain of them.

If Eliot's observation is correct, it is equally as true that the quality of our expectations determines our actions. As the semester unfolds, the quality of those expectations changes, often forcing us to make decisions about our students, decisions that mark certain of them as irretrievable.

They usually sit in the back of the room. They look at their watches in the middle of Plato's allegory of the case. After a recitation of Wittgenstein's death-bed admonition to "tell them all I've had a wonderful life," they inquire if this will be on the final exam.

There are students in each of my classes who, after fifteen weeks of Socratic method, hundreds of rhetorical questions, and a host of other cajoling techniques, have not uttered a single syllable.

This evening, now that it is over again, I wonder who these students are. I wonder about the expectations they had of me. I wonder what moves them at school, and in the dead of night. And I wonder about the intimacy I presumed when I told them what these philosophers we were studying together have done to me, how they have shaped my life, how they have made me become this odd man who wishes to stand before them for the purpose of asking just what it is they think is important.

This evening, after thirty-four semesters and sixteen summer sessions, I am searching for a metaphor about the arrival and departure of a teacher's expectations. I think I have found it in dancing.

In my classroom, I ask a number of students to dance; some stay by the folding chairs, away from the dance floor. They need to be coaxed into a waltz. Others willingly step forward, even when the steps are not entirely known. Still others, very quickly begin to lead. In a short while, they usually ask others out on the floor. And then there are the others: those who resolutely will not dance. They come underprepared. They don't wear their dancing shoes. They spend their time making knowing glances at each other, as if to say, "Aren't *they* making fools of themselves?" These students wouldn't be caught dead gliding across the floor with a good philosophical argument.

In one of his most beautiful essays, Emerson suggests that what we are more fundamentally, we are while teaching, not just voluntarily, but involuntarily. This is surely as true when we learn, and when we dance. In learning, no less than dancing, knowledge consists in understanding how to use the whole of oneself. This is just what many of my students will not do.

So now, this evening, after it is all over, I wonder if I should have been more persistent, if I should not have asked for a fourth and fifth time if they would care to dance. I wonder if I should not have told them of a Hindu proverb: Those who cannot dance often blame it on the floor.

*May, 1990*

# Writing About Writing:
## *Some Comments on Montaigne and the Essay*

I have never written about writing. I have always thought of that task as a self-referential paradox of sorts, something akin to the philosophical barber's dilemma: the barber shaves all those who don't shave themselves, so who shaves the barber? The writer writes about all those who don't write about themselves. Who writes about the writer? I am tempted to answer, "No one, and surely not the writer."

This is the kind of conundrum I could spend entire afternoons pondering in my grade school years. The old forest green and pumpkin yellow Crayola crayon box had a little boy on the front. He wore an earnest smile on his yellow face. He lifted a Crayola crayon box so it nearly touched his grinning cheek. On that box was a small boy wearing an earnest smile. He lifted a Crayola crayon box so it nearly touched his grinning cheek. And on that box was a still smaller child...

Sometimes on Saturdays I meandered around the house. I would dress exactly like the series of progressively smaller Crayola crayon boys, all grinning in the direction of infinity. I would hold my box of crayons so it nearly touched my grinning cheek. As I approached them, my sisters, for the briefest of moments, would look up from their Barbie dolls, but then immediately return to the conversation they were constructing between Barbie and her friend, Midge. I would hold the box and exclaim, "See!" They didn't see.

In that moment of rejection, I wondered if God might have a sense of humor, and if perhaps at that very moment he might be holding an enormous Crayola crayon box, a wry smile fixed on his cosmic face.

Writing about writing is much the same. It gives me that same feeling of vertigo I get when looking at a Rubik's cube or at monkeys in the zoo. Like the Rubik's cube, there is too much concentration in too small a place. There is too great a pressure to fit too many disparate pieces into too recognizable a shape. Writing about writing reminds me of looking at monkeys because the line of demarcation between the show and the audience is never sufficiently clear.

The essayist is perhaps in the greatest danger of becoming a self-referential paradox. He is already congenitally predisposed to believing that all he thinks about is interesting—that others are amused by the conversations he has with himself. If anyone should refrain from writing about writing it should be the essayist.

Yet, the greatest of the essayists, Michel de Montaigne, tells us, "Because I had nothing else to write about, I presented myself as a subject." He began this self-analysis out in the open, for all of us to see, in 1568 with the writing of his first essay. In fact, with that essay, Montaigne invented the genre. He informs us that when be began this little project the goal was not particularly clear. It is for this reason he chose to call them *essais,* "tests" or "trials." By 1588, he had completed three volumes of these short pieces.

What saved Montaigne from becoming a self-referential paradox, I think, was that there were so many of him locked up in the hollow of his head. Plato thought the mind was like a debating society. His was a wonderful description of Montaigne. "There is as much difference between us and ourselves as between us and others," remarked Montaigne, the former mayor of Bordeaux. He adds, "We are, I know not how, double in ourselves, so that what we believe we disbelieve, and cannot rid ourselves of what we condemn."

For Montaigne, and most of the other good essayists as well, multiple personalities lounge around in the vacant space of a single head, like cab drivers sitting around the garage waiting for the next fare from the dispatcher. There is no telling who will get the next ride. There is no telling how far the fare may want to go. Satirist, poet, historian, philologist, investigative reporter, comic, crazy person, all wait their turn to push the red flag on Montaigne's meter.

F. Scott Fitzgerald in *The Last Tycoon* points out that writers are not exactly people. If they are any good, they are a whole bunch of people trying hard to be one person. This is perhaps the best description of the successful essayist.

What all of Montaigne's voices have in common is a kind of love, a sad admiration for what is beautiful and transitory in life. Montaigne realized, better than any other essayist, that it is often the smallest of moments that deserves to be written down. The actual experience often lasts no longer than the width of an eyelash, so it is important to recreate it outside of time, in some unforgettable and eternal space—black words on a white line.

In the very best of Montaigne's essays, a voice becomes *the* voice for the smallest parcel of time. The transitory nature of the writing self becomes matched by the fleeting nature of the subject matter; a love springs quickly and deeply between the two. It can be shared by the reader. Long after the writer is gone, the words stand on the page like a monument to the marriage of fine prose to a vital moment.

For Montaigne, these vital moments need not be the most profound. His essays are sometimes funny or poetic, self-revelatory or sardonic, full of melancholy or sublime nonsense. But whatever he attempts to do, he always does it in the right voice. Montaigne knew that the sorting out of the voices was the real work of the essayist, and that the sorting out came in the form of syntax. *A* voice is transformed into *the* voice by the right size and shape of the sentence.

E.B. White, in a lovely preface to one of his books of essays, points out that the only real obligation of the essayist is to be honest about which of the voices he is using. He cannot indulge himself in conceit or concealment. Essays fail for many reasons but this is perhaps the greatest: the writer makes a bad decision about the person he wants to be in a piece of writing. When an essayist uses the wrong voice, it is like trying to breathe from another's lungs.

Montaigne quite unselfconsciously quotes Virgil, Horace, Martial and Dante. He informs us, "I quote others only better to express myself." *Precis* comes at a time when we mark the 400th anniversary of the publication of Montaigne's essays. Like Montaigne, you will find the writers of these pieces quoting Homer, Chekhov, Kierkegaard, Kollwitz, Forster, Tennyson, and Einstein. But each is written in its own distinctive voice. Each voice you will find here attempts to uncover a little piece of the truth. Montaigne knew something of the importance of finding that truth for oneself: "We can be knowledgeable with another's knowledge but we cannot be wise with another's wisdom."

*January, 1989*

# Mencken, a Life

"The gaseous Vertebrata who own, operate and affect the universe," H.L. Mencken wrote in one of his three autobiographical works, "have treated me with excessive politeness." If one judges that Baltimore's most famous literary citizen was correct in assessing his treatment at the hands of the gods, we must add that, in general, Vincent Fitzpatrick has been equally kind to the ghost of Henry Mencken.

*H.L. Mencken* is 153 pages of meticulous scholarship, written in a crisp and straightforward style. Working within a small book format, Fitzpatrick wisely chooses a chronological structure. He begins with a biographical overview followed by two chapters on Mencken's work up to the publication in 1919 of the first edition of *The American Language,* Mencken's most productive and influential period, and shorter chapters on the '30s and '40s. Newspaperman and playwright Ben Hecht, called Mencken of the 1920s "the Republic's one-man renaissance. More recently, Tom Wolfe suggested that the 1920s was the period when "American literature commuted from 1524 Hollins St.," Mencken's home for all but six years of his life.

Fitzpatrick concurs. Despite the fact that Fitzgerald, Hemingway and Faulkner were plying their trade at the same time, it was Sinclair Lewis and Mencken who dominated the American literary scene of the 1920s. Yet, Fitzpatrick judiciously points to Mencken's failure as a critic to recognize the importance of Fitzgerald's *Great Gatsby* and Theodore Dreiser's *An American Tragedy,* among other works. Though he championed some writers of merit, such as Joseph Conrad, Mencken's critical range was often excessively narrow and his taste sometimes deplorable.

Fitzpatrick's treatment of Mencken as social critic is less critical. He praises Mencken's *Treatise on the Gods* and its companion volume, *Treatise on Right and Wrong,* two books bound together by social Darwinism and a sophomoric philosophical tone. Fitzpatrick finds considerably more in these books than is there.

Mencken had a life-long war with professors. "No intelligent student ever learns much from the average drover of undergraduates, what he actually carries away came out of textbooks, or is the fruit of his own reading and inquiry," he wrote. The brilliant high-school educated Mencken regularly disparaged the possibility of American colleges turning out liberally educated people. But Mencken's more purely philosophical works point to how easy it is, even for a brilliant reader, without the aid of an experienced guide, to misrepresent great philosophical minds.

Fitzpatrick accomplishes much in a small space and thus sometimes suffers from imprecision: Mencken wrote forty-six books, not "in excess of 30"; Mencken tells us in the opening paragraph of *In the Footsteps of Gutenberg* that he received his much-discussed printing press on November 26, 1887, at the age of seven. Fitzpatrick says he was eight.

These are minor glitches for a man who has attempted to paint the visage of a richly talented and abundantly quirky character in a space the size of a postage stamp.

*June, 1989*

# The Whole Megilla

The other morning I was teaching the philosophy of Baruch Spinoza to my early class. In an attempt to explain the all-encompassing nature of the great Jewish thinker's metaphysical theory of monads, I completed my analysis by punctuating it with, "And thus Spinoza explains the whole megilla."

The word *megilla,* as you may know, is associated with a very lengthy ancient Hebrew religious text. In later years, because of the length of the *megilla,* the word came to mean anything of great size. My students at this small Catholic women's college didn't get the message. One can always tell when that happens. They get a glassy look in their eyes, like someone forced to listen to a graduation address over ten minutes in length.

I tried another level of analysis. "The whole megilla," I pointed out, "is bigger than the whole nine yards, or the whole shooting match. It is roughly equivalent to the whole smear, while being somewhat larger than the whole enchilada. In short, we are talking, more or less, about the whole ball of wax, if you know what I mean." They didn't know what I meant.

By now my students had forgotten about Spinoza, and they were not exactly appreciative of the enormity of the topic at hand, so it was then I raised a related philosophical question that has plagued me for years. When one uses the expression, "the whole kit and kaboodle," what exactly is "kaboodle?" And when one says "the whole kit and kaboodle," is it half kit and half kaboodle, or is it a little kit and a lot of kaboodle, or is there a preponderance of kit with just a tad of kaboodle?

What is the relationship between the whole megilla and the whole kit and kaboodle? Is it possible to get them mixed-up, so that we might have the whole kit and megilla, or the whole megilla and kaboodle, while the kit stands off longingly in the wings, the victim of an unrequited kaboodle?

We explored the nuances of these very difficult questions for nearly an hour. Finally, one student seemed to get it, a faint ray of comprehension spread across her features. "Will all this be on the final exam," she inquired. "The whole shebang," I said.

They all seemed instantly to understand.

*April, 1987*

# Dropping a Rose Petal

Don Marquis once remarked that publishing a book of poems is like dropping a rose petal down the Grand Canyon and waiting for the echo. A few weeks past, I had the pleasure of sitting in a small book-lined room at the Kelmscott shop where Josephine Jacobsen, former poetry consultant to the Library of Congress and fellow of the prestigious Academy of American Poets, read selections from her latest collection of poems, *The Sisters*.

Outside the book shop, people waited for buses that never came, a couple browsed in a deserted used car lot, and others walked their skinny dogs past this small row house where a few dozen people had gathered to listen to the echo of exquisite rose petals dropped from a giant height.

Jacobsen began with "The Chinese Insomniacs," a poem that demonstrates the often illusory nature of time and place. She told us of two Chinese poets born 900 years apart. Both share the blessing/curse of insomnia:

> A date is only a mark
> on paper—it has little to do
> with what is long.
> It is good to have their company
> tonight: a lady, awake
> until birdsong;
> a gentleman who made
> poems later out of frag-
> ments of the dark.

I wondered about the thirty or so people gathered together in this small room—older women, faculty members, too few students. I wondered more about all those who did not come. It tells us something, perhaps, about the state of American poetry, and about what is and is not so important in the remainder of a world that begins on 25th Street. Cyril Connolly wrote some time ago that most people do not believe in much of anything these days. Our greatest poetry is given to us by those who do.

We learn, as the reading unfolded, that there is much in which Jacobsen believes, but it does not resemble what passes for faith these days. It is more akin to Pascal or Kierkegaard, where God can be found just on the edge of tragedy. She reveals something of the mysteries to which she assents in "The Monosyllable." The poem is read in a strong, clear voice, larger and fuller than the poet's small frame might suggest:

> ...With it, she said,
> I may,
> if I can,
> sleep; since I must,
> die.
> Some say,
> rise.

Between poems, she talked briefly about the imperceptibility of change—of that day in June when summer seems like it has finally arrived and yet we now turn inescapably toward winter. In this life where change is so elusive, memory becomes one of our most precious possessions. In "The Rich Old Women" she reminds us of the "threadbare young" in their "thin small memories." She asks us to "bless them, and pity; you tell them, Turn Rich." Outside four young men walked past with a large boom box blaring.

Jacobsen ended with a lovely poem, "Gentle Reader." It is meant, of course, as homage to those who have come before her, to those who know with Paul Valery that in

145

poetry everything which *must* be said is almost impossible to say well. But in her poems Jacobsen regularly does the impossible:

> ...O God, it peels me, juices like a press;
> this poetry drinks me, eats me, gut and marrow
> until I exist in it jester's sorrow,
> until my juices feed a savage sight
> that runs along the lines, bright
> as beast's eyes. The rubble splays to dust:
> city, book, bed, leaving my ear's lust
> saying like Molly, yes, yes, O yes.

*May, 1988*

# Blessed Rage for Order Forms

*A place for everything, everything in its place.*
—Benjamin Franklin

*Chaos often breeds life, when order breeds habit.*
—Henry Adams

I sometimes do a little moonlighting at one of the local public universities. I was visiting there a few days ago with the philosophy department's secretary. In the midst of our chat I happened to glance down at her neatly kept desk to discover a blank form marked, in big black lettering, "University Order Form." Always fascinated by official looking documents and other people's business, I asked my friend exactly what one orders with the University Order Form. Without the slightest bit of hesitation, like a waiter pointing to the men's room before the patron has asked, the secretary answered, "Order Forms."

She was telling the truth. Upon further inspection, I discovered that one might order standard campus order forms, departmental order forms, SP (small purchase) order forms, and a variety of stationery order forms, all with the University Order Form.

But on still further analysis, it became clear the matter is not that simple. I know this because I read the small print marked, "Instruction for Ordering." It was there I discovered that in order to order the University Order Form with which I may order the campus order forms, the departmental order forms, the stationery order forms, or some SP (small purchase) order forms, I must attach a sample order form to the University Order Form when ordering.

But the instructions for ordering do not make it clear whether I should attach a sample University Order Form or a sample standard campus order form to my University Order Form when ordering. Brenda, the secretary, says it depends on whether I am ordering the University Order Form, the departmental order form, the stationery order form, the standard campus order form, or the SP (small purchase) order form. "Ordinarily," she said, "you attach the particular order form you are ordering, as a sample order form, to the University Order Form."

This all seemed to make perfectly good sense until I asked her what happens when one runs out of University Order Forms. "There would be no order form to which one could attach the sample order form. Wouldn't that tend to put the entire process out of order, so to speak?"

"Not at all," she said evenly. "If you had read more carefully the instructions for ordering you would know it is possible to give a verbal order or even a rush order in place of the University Order Form, as long as you send a written order along later after you've reordered. That way you never have to wait inordinately."

At the top of the University Order Form I discovered two empty boxes. At the top of the boxes is printed, "For Office Use Only." I said to Brenda, "What are these two empty boxes for at the top of the University Order Form?" "I'm not really sure," she responded, "I think those little boxes help the Ordering Department keep things in order."

Samuel Johnson one remarked, "Order is a lovely nymph, the child of beauty and wisdom; her attendants are comfort, neatness, and activity; her abode is the valley of happiness; she is always to be found when sought for." Dr. Johnson didn't tell you she can be found in the philosophy department. Her name is Brenda.

*March, 1988*

# The Eclectic Chair

When I was hired six years ago for my present position, it was as the chair*man* of the philosophy department. There is no real boast in this admission. The truth of the matter is that the other members of my department are older and much wiser than I, so they thought it would be a splendid idea to install me as chairman so that I might see to the awesome responsibilities of scheduling, filling out forms from the dean's office, and making sure the trash cans are emptied on a regular basis.

A few years after I arrived at this post, amid very earnest discussion about sexist language and androgynous alternatives, I was changed from a chair*man* to a chair*person*. The surgery was not painful. The process was a kind of benign version of the story of Peter Abelard. I went to sleep one evening as a chairman, I arrived in my office the following morning as a chairperson. Hardly anyone but my closest friends noticed the difference.

A few years later, it happened again. Along with my fellow chairpeople I was changed from a chairperson to a chair. This, of course, is the stuff of which Kafka's short stories are made. A suitably angst-ridden Czechoslovakian named Gregor goes to bed one evening only to discover the following morning he has been transformed into a gigantic piece of furniture. Back in the real world the logic that went along with the movement from person to inanimate object went something like this: the word *chairperson* is too cumbersome to fit on small quarter-page memos. The solution was to "drop the person part."

For the last couple of years I have been trying to figure out what kind of chair I might be. I was thinking about this the other day during the meeting of the departments' chairs. (This should not be confused with the department's chairs, which are mostly wooden and swivel.) At the meeting of the departments' chairs, the chairs sit around on boardroom chairs and talk with the dean, who is sort of the chair of the chairs, so she is required to chair the chairs' meeting.

I thought for a while I might be a wing chair. There is something interesting and mythic about a wing chair. It reminds me of Ikaros. If Ikaros were a chair, he would certainly be a wing chair. Later, I imagined I would be a Chippendale, but I really do not have the legs for it. My Marxist friends believed I might be a Castro convertible, but I have not been politically active since college. Some other friends suggested I might be a bent-wood rocker or possibly a La-Z-Boy, but I think they were just being un-*chair*itable.

This afternoon I spent some time in my office musing about this problem of chair identity. I rocked back and forth on my wooden swivel chair. It made those wonderful creaking noises like certain ominous African insects or a tone-deaf but maniacally persistent soprano might make. I tried to make those creaking sounds. All of my much older and wiser department members closed their office doors. It soon became clear I am not a wooden swivel chair.

This entire experience began to make me feel like a beanbag chair, like I had no real substance, no backbone, no genuine sense of identity. I thought the only thing to do was to become a folding chair. But then, in the midst of my office with its piles of books and papers, forms from the dean's office, and the large metal trash can filled to overflowing with discarded ideas, offers from the Publisher's Clearing House, and unsalable prose, it occurred to me: what I really want to be known as is an eclectic chair.

This should not be confused with the *electric* chair.

*February, 1987*

# Reunion and the Problem of Change

I spent Friday morning talking with my students about two ancient Greek philosophers, Parmenides and Heraclitus. The two are known today, 2,500 years later, for a debate over what in their time was a pressing issue—the problem of change.

Parmenides came to the rather startling conclusion that nothing changes, while Heraclitus insisted there is nothing permanent except change. It is not surprising that it is Heraclitus and not Parmenides who is known as the "weeping philosopher."

I thought about Heraclitus on Saturday evening. I went to my twentieth high school reunion. It was held in the school cafeteria. Men approaching forty walked around with yearbook photos, taken two decades ago, pinned to their chests—much needed evidence that they were the same people as the boys staring from those graduation photos. In my photo my ears hang on the sides of my skinny face like the open doors of my father's 1961 Chevrolet Biscayne.

At the reunion, wives stood around in clusters benignly listening to athletic accomplishments both real and imagined. Men traded stories of late adolescent cleverness and cruelty. I left after an hour.

After the first few minutes, I had begun to get a sinking feeling, like sitting in a train at the station and not knowing for sure whether it was the train or the platform that suddenly had started to move.

After we left the celebration, a friend and I sat in my garden and talked about the problem of change. We had gone together to my tenth reunion. In the meantime, she has gone through career changes, a divorce, and the raising of her son from a first grader to a high school lacrosse star. My changes have been less public, more subtle. The twentieth reunion had a much more sobering effect than the tenth.

Afterwards, in the garden, the last of the roses were falling from their stems. The moon had moved from wax to wane, and Saturday night had mysteriously given birth to Sunday morning.

It was in the garden I suddenly understood that college teaching is a profession where one easily becomes lulled into believing that Parmenides is right—that nothing changes. Each September produces a new collection of faces in my classroom. They are as young as last year's students. They ask the same questions as the year before, and the year before, and the year before.

And if these faces do not change, and if the questions do not change, then surely Parmenides is right.

But earlier in the evening, in that high school cafeteria, a room now half the size of twenty years ago, I looked across a formica table top at men entering the second half of their lives—hardworking men with mortgages and bills from the orthodontist. These were faces changed by the gain and loss of love, by weddings, anniversaries, first communions, and funerals, and by a war that was never called a war. These were faces shaved some 4,000 times since our glances last met.

Later, in the garden, I thought about Marcel Proust's observation in *Remembrance of Things Past* that we do not succeed in changing things according to our desires, but gradually it is our desires themselves that change. John Locke believed it was continuity of memory that constitutes the enduring self. But sometimes the memory finds little room for old desires. It was the difficulty in capturing my old desires, an inability to find twenty-year-old dreams I might still wish to keep, that created my uneasiness at the reunion.

By the end of the evening, I understood that it is Heraclitus, the weeping philosopher, who is correct. The only sense that is common in the long run is the sense of change—and most of us instinctively avoid it.

*October, 1988*

# On Hand Raising

The other day I was reminded of how college students raise their hands in class. In one of my introductory courses a student placed her right elbow on the flat surface of her desk and proceeded to waive her ballpoint pen in a faint circular motion, as if trying to draw very small circles in the air above her inverted pen. This was a sign for me, her instructor, that she had a question. I have taught long enough that this one was not a difficult call.

Sometimes it is not so easy. Students who raise their pens to half-mast, dangling them at about ten o'clock high, are much more difficult to figure. If the pen moves to nine o'clock, the question or comment disappears. When it approaches eleven o'clock I consider it a *bona fide* attempt at communication.

Students who twirl their fingers in their hair are just as difficult to read. One moment it looks like a question, the next a simple case of the heartbreak of psoriasis.

I have only lately come to understand that this business of hand raising is a real barometer of what is and is not happening in our schools. When these students who now sit before me were swinging their feet nervously below their seats and above the floor of their third-grade classrooms, they posed and answered questions in a very different way—their little arms shot out at a forty-five degree angle. When elbows locked into place, it produced in them a persistent little sound, delicate, plaintive, and meant for the teacher: "Oooh! Oooh! Choose me, choose me."

They continued their oohing for what seemed the longest of times, their entire bodies stretching forward, fingers dancing at the teacher, until all that remained on their desk seats was that single, obligatory knee.

The teacher stood before this waving sea of eager hands and minds like a Nebraska wheat farmer in the middle of his bumper crop on a windswept day. But the teacher too often looked for that one embarrassed student whose seed had not yet grown to a waving stalk.

After a few more minutes of oohing, the student grain began to undulate with less energy, their heavy heads plopping on their wooden desks. But the truly diligent among them managed to keep their hands raised nevertheless. The elbows of their free arms were planted firmly on their desks, while their hands added much needed support for the wavers now heavy with fatigue. The oohing grew fainter and fainter until persistence gave way to limb exhaustion and a well-learned lesson on the value of intellectual curiosity.

Over the next few years it would get much worse. By their second year of high school many students had learned a painful lesson: raising one's hand, even when still interested, was about as desirable as a bad case of zits. By this time, showing real enthusiasm for Shakespeare, Euclid, or how DNA creates life with its tiny spiral staircases of nucleic acid, is decidedly removed from the realm of cool.

A few years later, they sit before me, not really sure any longer of the ground rules. Those few who are getting their philosophy courses "out of the way" find little use for questions about the nature of the soul or how to judge a good argument, or a good person, when they see one. They are like small frogs who think their puddle is a giant sea. These few students sit in the back of the room. They look at their watches like lonely travelers waiting for a hopelessly delayed train.

But there are also many braver souls—those who raise index fingers hesitantly to the height of collar bones. They sometimes sheepishly glance from side to side, as if concerned about being caught in the act.

I make these students raise their whole hand—and high. I am working on them so that they might exclaim "oooh, ooh, ooh!" when they do it.

*November, 1989*

# On Visiting Poe with Borges

I learned of the death of Jorge Luis Borges while standing at the check-out desk of the Yale Divinity School library. I had brought a brittle, yellow copy of the Hebrew Bible to the librarian to see if it might be taken home. While I waited my turn, a young man asked about a book on Pythagoras. I glanced down at a copy of the *New York Times* folded on the counter. When I flipped it over, the paper opened to the obituaries. In the corner of the page the wall-eyed gaze of a blind man stared back. It was Jorge Luis Borges.

I had been introduced to Borges on a cold afternoon a few years before. He had come to Baltimore to speak at Johns Hopkins, but I met him at the tomb of Edgar Allan Poe.

On the morning I learned of Borges' death, I opened the fragile Hebrew text and ran my blind finger down a random page until it stopped. When I opened my eyes, the nail of my right index finger had come to rest at the end of Deuteronomy, at the account of Moses' funeral.

In one of Borges' stories, "The Secret Miracle," the hero dreams he has concealed himself in one of the naves of the Clementine Library. A blind librarian asks him, "What are you looking for?" The hero answers, "I am looking for God." The librarian responds, "God is in one of the letters on one of the pages of one of the 400,000 volumes of the Clementine." Later, Hladik, the hero, finds the letter by accident.

The Yale librarians informed me the Hebrew text was much too brittle to take home, so I left without it. On the steps I remembered that the afternoon I met with Borges he said there are no accidents—only an inability to understand the causes. I acted a little skeptical. He quoted impeccably from Boethius' *De Consolatione Philosophiae,* where a spectator is in the hippodrome and sees, from his box, the unfolding of a horse race. He sees it from start to dramatic finish. But Boethius, Borges pointed out, also imagines a second observer. This is the spectator who sees the entire race in an instant. "This spectator, of course," said Borges, "is God."

A few minutes earlier, we had been to Poe's original burial place, in the family plot in the rear of the Westminster Cemetery. Borges ran his fingers along the burial stone until they stopped at the raven cut into the top of the smooth grey marble. The old man spoke, "I might have suspected this" and went on to recite:

> *But the Raven, sitting lonely on the placid bust, spoke only that one word, as if his soul in that one word he did outpour.*
> *Nothing farther then he uttered—not a feather then he fluttered—*
> *Till I scarcely more than muttered "Other friends have flown here before."*
> *Then the bird said "Nevermore."*

We meandered around the rest of the cemetery: an obscure American philosophy professor and a blind Argentine legend. We talked about Melville and Twain, Kierkegaard and Dante. He asked me what sort of bug Gregor Samsa turned into. Borges voted for something called an Egyptian dung beetle. Above our heads, grey clouds moved swiftly by. A few breaks in the clouds appeared, revealing a deep blue sky behind. It was like a giant sea peered at through a series of mysteriously moving windows.

Throughout the afternoon I stared at Borges. It was as if I expected him somehow to look more ethereal than he did: thin, nearly white hair, slicked back; much taller than I had imagined. His right eye looked straight ahead as if trying to see something at a great distance. His left eye was fixed lower in the socket than its partner. It perpetually looked down probing the ground for something lost:

*I know the things I've lost are so many that I
could not begin to count them
and that those losses
now, are all I have.*

Borges said that when he was a child he had always been terrified of mirrors. He remarked that Poe must have felt that way too. "There is a neglected essay of Poe's," he went on to tell me, "on the decoration of rooms." One of the conditions Poe insisted on is that the mirror be placed in such a way that a seated person not be reflected. Borges suggested the use of the double in "William Wilson" and the idea for "The Narrative of Arthur Gordon Pym" were related to this fear.

A few moments of silence passed. I listened to his uneven breathing as I formulated my next question. "Are you afraid of death?" He answered as if the question had been posed a thousand times. "When writers die they become books. This is not a bad incarnation, is it?"

Twenty years after Poe's death his body was moved from the family plot in the rear of the graveyard to a place of honor just inside the gates. Pennies collected from Baltimore schoolchildren paid for the impressive white marble monument beneath which his bones now rest.

Borges approached the monument. He placed his cane in the crook of his right arm. His fingers ran across the bronze relief of Poe's face which juts out of the side of the white stone. The old man looked at me with those blind eyes, one looking down in the direction of those moldering bones, the other peering out as if to catch a fatal glimpse of the river Styx. Finally, the old poet spoke: "This is the Edgar I know."

In a cemetery in Argentina, beneath a modest stone, the body of Jorge Luis Borges has slept for nearly two years. Before his death, he returned to the writing of poetry:

*In the night there will be no star,*
*There will be no night.*
*I will die and with me the sum*
*of the intolerable universe.*
*I will erase the pyramids, the medals,*
*the continents and the faces.*
*I will ease the accumulation of the past.*
*I will make dust of history, dust of dust.*
*I am looking at the last sunset.*
*I hear the last bird.*
*I will be nothingness to no one.*

It was like Borges to end on the wonder of a double negative.

*April, 1988*

# Finding the Words

I have never owned a camera. With the exception of obliging a persistent pair of Japanese tourists in front of Buckingham Palace, I have not taken a single photograph. As a writer, I have secretly preferred to think of myself as not needing a camera. I have held a view that when writing is at its best it turns inside out the old adage that a picture is worth a thousand words. In the very best of writing, a few words can be worth more than a thousand pictures.

Paul Theroux, travel writer, novelist, and another man who does not own a camera, prefers to think of the writer's eye as a camera lens, and the mind's eye as photographic film. What we see, he suggests, gets imprinted in memory, that everchanging but natural photo album.

Essay writing is like taking photographs. But in the making of an essay something unusual happens between the clicking of the shutter and the development of the image. The "unusual something" is the interposing of language and experience just where they are most needed, between event and essay. Sometimes the developing of the image comes like in an insta-matic; one waits thirty seconds and it is ready. I have been waiting patiently in my darkroom for thirty-five years for other pictures to dry.

For a long time, I have searched for a metaphor, a simile that might convey the power and frustrations of the essayist. I do not think I have found it in Theroux's camera. Even among the best of photographers, the camera still does much of the work. The essayist may wait Zen-like for the pen to produce, but the pen sits silently, defiantly, never once providing as much as a conjunction or participle.

My photographer friends tell me one must decide between taking the photograph or having the experience. One is sacrificed for the other in a kind of Sophie's choice or Kierkegaardian either/or. But the essayist rarely finds himself in this kind of dilemma. Almost never is he forced to make a choice about what must be lost. In a real way, the essayist asks the girl to the prom the night after it is over. She usually accepts. They almost always have a wonderful time.

There is also another reason for abandoning the essayist-as-camera metaphor. When we describe ourselves as machines, even very complicated ones, something deeply mysterious (and thus deeply sacred) is lost. We turn simile to analog. We make printouts of poetry.

Every age seems to invent metaphors and similes for explaining the mystery of the self and its fascination with recovering the past. These days the grand metaphor for memory goes something like this: The mind, or still worse, the brain, is like a computer and memory is like data stored on floppy disks.

In the eighteenth century, just after European gentlemen began carrying pocket watches, the mind was thought to resemble a grand timepiece, precise, orderly, and working in a complex teleology.

But the mind is only *like* a watch or a computer, for it is in the very nature of a metaphor to hide as much as it reveals. Watches and computers cannot veil a truth, or even change one. It is in the very stuff of the human being to do so. It is sometimes in the reinvention of the past, a past out of order or place, where the essayist can be found at his best.

I have come to realize that the making of essays is more like giving directions than anything else. Some listeners have been to the destination before, others travel there for the first time. The essayist must convince the latter that the trip is worthwhile. He must be honest enough with the former that the experience is recognized as a mutual one worth revisiting.

But even this new image—the essayist as giver of directions—is not enough. My resistance to it, as well as the camera simile, has its roots in my inabilities as a writer. Some of those inadequacies are mine alone, others exist in anyone who has put pen to paper or incriminating fingerprints on word-processing keys.

We practice a craft where, unlike the photograph, the finished product is rarely as beautiful as the original. I have tried to find words to express a feeling that comes with the sight of white doves spilling from the bell tower of a medieval Scottish university, or the sense of numbing pain etched on the faces of street people huddled around a city steam grate on a biting cold February morning. We give directions. We get our listeners as close as we can to the sacred place. But out instructions are hardly ever enough. The words are rarely as beautiful, as serene, as terrifying as they ought to be.

One day in the Sahara, many years ago, I waited for hours in the dark, staring toward the east, waiting for that first instant of sunrise in which a sliver of rose-colored light turns dark sand the color of old newspapers.

It only happens in that moment. An eye blink means another failure. When one sees it, it is like finding the words. It is like being a writer.

*June, 1990*

# Travel

*A traveler without observations is like a bird without wings.*
—S<small>AADI</small>

# From Baltimore to Baltimore

Paul Theroux, the noted travel writer and novelist, once remarked that travel is glamorous only in retrospect. Theroux never rode the bus. Even after you have been there, it is difficult to find anything glamorous about Effingham, Illinois. Effingham. It sounds like the punch line of a dirty joke. For three weeks this summer I stopped in Effingham and eighty-two other cities and towns across America, while leaving the driving to Greyhound.

Even after deregulation of the airline industry, travel in the friendly skies is magic. One buckles in and forgets. You wake up several hours later and it is yesterday again. Anything notable in air travel is disastrous. Tolerable periods of boredom are punctuated by the momentary terror of take-off and landing. On an airplane the measurement of time is supersonic. It moves faster than the plane itself.

Travel by bus is a different, more painful story. The hands of the clock move there as for inmates doing hard time. On the bus there is the everpresent feeling of being held captive. There is a good bit of loathing and fear. For the experienced traveler there is the nagging suspicion that seated somewhere on your bus is a human time bomb. God or DNA, or some other of the powers that be, has decided that at some specific moment in the unfortunate life of this person his head will explode so that there is one small piece of him for each of the inhabitants of China. The veteran bus traveler's only hope is that it not happen in the seat next to his.

In one of his notebooks, Albert Camus points out that what gives value to travel is fear:

> It is a fact that at a certain moment, when we are so far from home, we are seized by a vague fear, and an instinctive desire to go back to the protection of old habits. This is the most obvious benefit of travel. There is no pleasure. I look upon it more as an occasion for spiritual testing.

Occasions for spiritual testing came frequently on the Greyhound this summer: eighty-three departures and arrivals. Eighty-two were late.

In *Death Comes to the Archbishop,* Willa Cather suggests, "Men travel faster now, but I do not know if they go to better things." Greyhound buses do not travel faster. I leave it to you to decide if I have gone to better things.

・ ・ ・

There is no polite way to describe the inside of a bus station. They are always smoke-filled imitations of the unemployment office, a free medical clinic, or the visitor's room at a state prison. What these places share are people on whose faces gravity and tragedy have conspired to make them old before their time.

Orange shell seats are bolted together in orderly rows, their occupants wedded indissolubly in a confraternity of listlessness. Travelers, street people, hustlers, and the insane, all sit in these orange shell seats, looking like bands of narcoleptics trying to serve on jury duty.

There are only two items in all of reality made of that orange day-glo plastic: bus station seats and cafeteria trays. When bus station seats fall apart, they get melted down into cafeteria trays. When the cafeteria trays wear out, they are heated until they bubble, and then fashioned into brand new bus station seats. The whole process works according to Newtonian physics: matter is neither created nor destroyed, it merely changes into bus station seats.

・ ・ ・

The new Baltimore Greyhound terminal is situated in something called the Travel Plaza. From the outside, it looks like an airport terminal, lots of glossy orange brick, chrome and glass. On the inside, it looks like a bus station: a large, smoke-filled room full of lost souls and orange shell seats.

I bought my ticket ($260 for three weeks of unlimited travel) and found a seat in the waiting room. The man to my left looked middle-eastern. He wore lots of gold jewelry, and traveled with a cheap suitcase held together with a much larger man's belt. He was prematurely balding and had made that awesome decision that men in his position frequently do to keep adjusting the part so that it moved farther and farther south from the top of his head. By now it had creeped down to the border of his left ear. It was just a matter of time before the part would slip completely off his head. In the meantime, he was gallantly attempting, like some ill-zfated Saharan farmer, to ward off the inevitable.

To my right was a forty-five-year-old man with black frame glasses, blue jeans, and sideburns worn by midwestern farmers and men who have not quite gotten over Elvis' passing.

*Sideburns:* Well, you off today?
*Middle-eastern Badpart:* What?
*Sideburns:* You off today? When you gotta go to work?
*Middle-eastern Badpart:* I live on my investments.

We sat in the station from 1:45 to 2:45. I thought about what sort of investments a man sitting in a bus station with someone else's belt wrapped around his suitcase might have. Sideburns asked nine other men if they were off today.

. . .

At 2:45 the 1:45 bus to Pittsburgh arrived. Our operator was Joseph E. Leonard. I know it was Joseph E.

Leonard because the little sign above the driver's head was blank until Joseph E. Leonard placed his name tag in the slot between "Your Operator" and "safe, reliable, and courteous." Every Greyhound bus is equipped with this feature. Most of the drivers don't bother to slip their names between the job classification and the three immutable adjectives. In three weeks of travel, some drivers were tall, some short, some chatty and philosophical, some surly and uncooperative, but all were "safe, reliable, and courteous."

. . .

The station in Frederick, Maryland, is a small box of a building. The blue lockers that line the wall are twenty-five cents; the pay toilets are a dime. The rest rooms are for the convenience of ticketed customers only. A small woman with three enormous suitcases stood outside the building and screamed at a small boy named Jonathan.

We made a short stop in Hagerstown, where a portly woman in a flowered dress and white, summer sandals entered the bus and flopped down in the seat next to mine. Greyhound buses no longer have dividers or armrests between the seats. This creates a bit of a logistical problem for people seated next to the overweight. It is very difficult as well for the large people to sit comfortably on a long-distance bus. The woman next to me looked and breathed like a large aquatic mammal tragically washed ashore. My half of our shared space ebbed and flowed as she shifted her considerable weight.

The Catoctin mountains rose unobtrusively from the lush green hills of western Maryland. The hills are thickly populated with tall, straight trees. They stand almost in rows, like soldiers at attention on a parade ground. In the first seat behind Joseph E. Leonard sat a young man from California. He discussed his long-term career plans with a stranger who looked like Charles Manson.

We made a thirty-minute stop in Breezewood, Pennsylvania. The Post House Restaurant is decorated in an early American motif. Everywhere one looks, it's 1970s early American, except the video games.

Our driver from Breezewood to Pittsburgh was Tony Bafile. He was, of course, safe, reliable, and courteous. A woman across the aisle from me purchased a tabloid during the rest stop. *"I've been stalked by death," Vannah says after dad becomes fifth loved one to die; "Sexy critics of Stallone's wild wife." "Lose 16 pounds on a new diet for women over 35."* This article was accompanied by a photograph full of women holding placards announcing how much weight they have lost. One woman in the back of the group sheepishly holds up a 2.

Western Pennsylvania is full of winding roads and breathtaking valleys. Small towns full of Burger Kings and Pizza Huts dot the landscape. Outside of Somerset, the scene changes to flat farm land, red barns and rusting automobiles. A sleeveless man worked on an old Pontiac in front of the Somerset bus station. The tattoo on his left arm featured a dagger plunged through an appropriately bleeding heart, small drops of blue blood frozen on his bicep.

A bent-up little man entered the bus at Somerset. His clothes were much too big for him, as if he had been surprised by a jealous husband and left in a hurry with the wrong trousers and jacket. He found a seat beside the woman with the tabloid. He pulled a worn Bible from his pocket and read from the Song of Songs.

We made a stop in Monroeville, a suburban station outside of Pittsburgh. Naked mannequins stood unselfconsciously in the window of Wedding World. We were in Pittsburgh by 9:00 p.m.

I had decided before the trip began to spend my evenings either on night buses or in the hotel closest to the bus station. In Pittsburgh, it is the Weston William Penn, a beautiful, recently renovated, nineteenth-century building.

In the morning I arrived at the station at 11:00 for an 11:30 bus to Indianapolis. The Pittsburgh station is one of the most modern in the country. It features twenty doors for arrivals and departures, a Burger King built into the side of the building, and plastic shell seats in a variety of colors.

I sat at door number eleven. A small woman wearing a blond wig snapped her gum incessantly. A queue formed by 11:15. Behind me a man in a wrinkled summer suit shook uncontrollably on his right side. The woman with the gum looked at him and said, "Missah, can't you stop that shakin'?"

A small, tow-headed boy stood defiantly ten to twelve feet from his mother. Every ten to fifteen seconds the mother intoned, "Matthew, get over here." She did this about 150 times. Matthew stuck his tongue out at the woman. The thirty or forty people standing on line found this quite amusing. The woman did not.

The bus left Pittsburgh at 11:50. Outside my window A-frame houses appeared, and trees dry enough to look like autumn.

Charles Manson sat across the aisle. The shaking man discussed with him the state of American schools. The young woman next to me wore a camouflage jacket and listened to her walkman. I settled into Elledge's biography of E.B. White.

The Allegheny Mountains made their appearance outside Washington, Pennsylvania. We turned on Route 70 and headed toward Wheeling, West Virginia. The sign atop a Washington bank announced it was 100 degrees. This turned the inhabitants of the bus into instant thermal statisticians. Several people offered up stories of their hottest day on earth.

The station in Wheeling is in the business district. Next door, at Mr. William's House of Hair Fashion, Mr. William, unaware he had an audience, had pealed back his toupee and was toweling off his scalp when our bus pulled in.

A very large woman with several packages boarded the bus in Wheeling. When people move down the aisle with lots of carry-on baggage they rarely understand that behind them, in their wake, their packages usually bonk several unsuspecting passengers on the head. The woman felled about half a dozen travelers before she found her seat in the middle of the bus.

It was at about this time it occurred to Matthew that he had not disrupted the life of his long-suffering mother for nearly two hours. In order to remedy this situation, Matthew, realizing he had forty other innocent adults at his mercy as well, proceeded to scream like a coward in thumb-screws. Two French people seated behind me began speaking in their native tongue about infanticide.

Matthew screamed, loud and bug-eyed, all the way to Cambridge, Ohio. My atlas tells me it is a distance of sixty miles. It seemed much longer. Since I could no longer read, I began to think of devices I might invent for use in torturing this child. I finally settled on a simple and effective idea: a large silver hammer to be located next to the "safe, reliable, and courteous" sign. It could be held in a little fire-engine-red box with a sign that reads, "Break glass for child emergency."

· · ·

In Cambridge, Ohio, a heavy woman with a beautiful five-year-old girl boarded the bus. In a voice like the mothers on TV advertisements, the woman instructed the child to "sit next to the nice lady." The little girl found her seat beside the woman with the packages.

A few moments later a black man in the seat behind the driver teetered back toward the bathroom. ("This vehicle is equipped with a rest room for your convenience.") The man wore a blue Mexican shirt, pale blue cotton pants with a white vest, and untied running shoes. If the world moves at 45 rpms, this man was permanently stuck at 33 1/3. Each step was deliberate and carefully executed, like a high-wire artist, or a man on his way to the electric chair. When he reached the little girl's seat, the child said, "Here comes a black man." The mother responded with a slightly agitated TV voice, "Don't say that word." "What word?" "That word you just said." "Here comes a black man."

With this repetition, the man turned toward the tow-headed child and said, "What's a matter, whitey? You ain't never seen a black man?"

. . .

Just outside Columbus, Ohio, a motel sign reads: Waterbeds and Children Free.

The station in Columbus is a modern one-story building with a Burger King. In the center of the terminal is a large square area enclosed by a three-foot wooden wall. The area looks like a holding pen of some sort. Only ticketed passengers are allowed there. Around the inside perimeter of the pen are orange shell seats and coin-operated television sets.

Between Columbus and Springfield the portly women discussed their in-laws. In the middle of the conversation, the mother of the child admitted, "They're not here to defend themselves, so I guess I shouldn't talk about them." She does.

The package lady's husband is named Richard. She spoke as if Richard had been a dear friend to all of us.

The land between Columbus and Springfield is flat with few trees. About twelve miles outside of Springfield, we learned of Richard's problem with "the impotence."

After a short stop in the small stucco station at Springfield, we headed for Dayton. The young woman with the camouflage alighted at Springfield. As she swung around her seat she gave me the kind of wink one often gets from people who feel sorry for you.

The portly friends discussed smoking. The woman with the child used to weigh 102 pounds until she stopped smoking. Now she weighs 312 pounds. The other woman told all who were listening that she tips the scales at 400 pounds, "give or take a pound or two." They both had "glandular problems." Each fished into her large handbag to produce "thyroid pills," which they shook at each other.

• • •

In Dayton, Michael E. Banta became our driver. He was short, wore reflective sunglasses, and was "safe, reliable, and courteous."

In Dayton, a thin man with a Hawaiian shirt took the empty seat next to mine. He introduced himself as "Charles, as in Bore-Yeh." On his right foot was a desert boot. On his left foot, a running shoe. His baggage consisted of a large disposable diaper box held together with frayed cord. Charles as in Bore-Yeh held a small radio to his left ear. After an hour of silent traveling, he turned to me and spoke.

"Do *you* want to know a secret?"

"Sure," I said.

"God," there was a dramatic pause, "God speaks to *me* in *this* radio."

"What frequency is he on?" I asked.

"Oh, no," he responded quickly, "I asked *you* if you wanted to know *a* secret, not *two* secrets."

Outside my bus window the sun had just appeared from behind a huge cloud that looked like Popeye's profile.

• • •

I decided to spend the night in Richmond, Indiana, about sixty miles east of Indianapolis. The closest hotel to the station was a Knights Inn. The rug in my room was a purple shag. The drapes and bedspread were a matching purple velour. It looked like an Italian whore house.

In the morning I walked around Richmond. It is a small town of large Victorian houses, white wooden porches and older women in house dresses. It is dominated by Route 40 West which runs right through the middle of town. Hoagy Carmichel recorded "Star Dust" there; it was in Richmond that William Jennings Bryant gave his cross of gold speech; Richmond C.F. Jenkins, the man who invented the television set, lived there for most of his life. The roller skate was invented in Richmond. And in the 1930s and '40s it was known as the "lawn mower capital of the world." It is not clear why it was called the lawn mower capital of the world. Did they make more lawn mowers than any other city, or did they cut more lawns? It is also not clear who became the lawn mower capital of the world after Richmond relinquished the title. I thought this might still be a sore subject with the older residents of the city, so I didn't bring it up.

. . .

In the morning I boarded a bus for St. Louis. Two hours into the day's ride, two older men played gin across the aisle. Their wives sat behind them and talked about their grandchildren. The husbands are retired railroad workers. They have never ridden on a long-distance bus.

We stopped for lunch at a Burger King in Vaudolin, Illinois. The railroad husbands went to order as the wives spread Burger King napkins as placemats.

In the evening the sunset looked like Longfellow's magician "extending his golden wand o'er the landscape." A while later, gold has turned to indigo and magenta. We pulled into the Terre Haute station after dark. A young man stood alone in the station. He muttered over and over, to himself, or perhaps to me, "Who does that woman think she is?"

. . .

The closest hotel to the bus station in Terre Haute is a flop house. Women in fishnet stockings sat in a lobby filled with plastic plants. The large black man at the desk wore a name tag with "Ben" etched in its center. $12.40 for the night. Check out time 11:00 a.m. "Don't be late."

The room came as a great surprise: new sheets, clean bathroom, but a funny grey dust on the bathroom mirror. About 11:30 p.m. there was a light rap on the door. I looked through the peep hole to discover that, although I am 6'2", I was looking into the chest of the man on the other side of the door. "Open the door," a voice said from somewhere near the top of the door frame.

"You have to be kidding," I said.

"Come on man, open the door. I got somethin' important to tell you."

"Tell me through the door."

"I can't, man. Open the door."

When I opened the door, a black man, approximately 6'10" and 180 pounds stood before me, his head ducked through the frame.

"Do you know what?" he said, pointing his long index finger at my chest.

"No, what?" I said.

"There was a dead man in your bed last night."

"You have cleared up a very great mystery for me," said I, and I closed and locked the door.

I spent the evening reading the Gideon Bible and watching the neon lights change shape and color until there was light.

. . .

In the morning, I caught a bus to St. Louis. An hour later I was on my way to Tulsa, Oklahoma. I slept through much of central Missouri, where the terrain changes in the Ozarks to hills and sheer rock face against the roadway.

Meramec Caverns has 300 signs along the highway. After 299 reminders of what you can see—Jesse James' hideout, the wax museum, the beautiful caverns—the 300th sign says, "You just missed it."

The bus crossed over to Oklahoma about 4:00 p.m. The eastern part of the state is much greener than I imagined. Scenes from *Grapes of Wrath* have a way of substituting themselves for what is actually Oklahoma.

A small man with a pencil-thin mustache listened to a radio: "Bank failures in Oklahoma climb to 19 this year"; a young man shot and killed two workers in a Cuba, Missouri, convenience store. Another employee said that during the shootings, the assailant continually shouted that he was an angel of God. "Local psychiatrists have determined the man was suffering from mental problems." While pondering this great advance in forensic medicine, we pulled into the Tulsa terminal.

. . .

I spent the evening with friends who live in a Tulsa suburb. In the morning we drove to Oral Roberts University. In the center of campus is a large, recently constructed hospital, built when Mr. Roberts saw a 900-foot Jesus who commanded him to raise funds for the structure.

We parked in the "River of Life Parking Lot" (time limit: twenty minutes) and headed over to the Healing Center, a one-story multi-purpose building that houses Oral Roberts' "Walk Through the Bible." We were placed with a group of twenty students from a school for the deaf in northern Oklahoma.

After a brief introduction, our guide, a young red-headed woman named Carole, herded us into a darkened and empty room. We stood in the dark for a few moments until a baritone voice-over broke the silence: "LET THERE BE LIGHT!" This was accompanied by a beam of light that instantly cut across the darkness. This came as a very big surprise to the students from the deaf school because the darkness had precluded them from seeing their signer who had dutifully been doing the "Let there by light" part in the dark. As the voice-over continued to create things, a smoke machine and several back-lighted slide projectors were helping with the creation. The smoke machine created another insurmountable problem for the signer and his students.

When we got to the end of the chapter, we moved on to the second room, the garden of Eden. The room appeared to be your basic garden of Eden, except for a few minor innovations: the tree of life featured fruit that contained little electric light bulbs, which perhaps explains better the concept of original sin than any theological tract one might read. If you eat fruit that contains little electric light bulbs, it is bound to do something disastrous to one's progeny the other major improvement in Mr. Roberts' Eden is that the serpent has a decided lisp. "Oh, you're gonna love this fruit," the lizard intoned, in a voice resembling a marriage of the enunciation of Truman Capote to the cadence of Bella Lugosi. The whole incident was suitably frightening. We were allowed to see the sin, and then were herded down a long passageway that featured flailing arms and legs which stuck out of the walls. The appendages were accompanied by an uneven chorus of moans and screams. The screaming put the signer in another awkward position trying to explain to these twenty students moving briskly down a narrow hallway, that they were not exactly getting the full effect.

The hallway led to Noah's ark where we were subjected to a "simulated forty days and forty nights of rain." A small, very nervous girl to my right began showing all the signs of unsimulated motion sickness.

After the dove returned with an olive branch, we moved on to a small amphitheater, where Oral and Richard Roberts had a recorded message waiting for us. The gist of the message was that Oral and Richard love "each and everyone of us," and so does God.

Those people with "special healing needs" were urged to seek an Oral Roberts' prayer partner for a $15 donation. While the folks from the deaf school were plunking down their fives and tens, I caught up with Carole. "Excuse me," I said, as I touched her elbow from behind. (It had not occurred to me until that moment just how much she looked like Eve.) "I was wondering...the hallway...with the screaming arms and legs...does it have a name?"

"The way of say-yin," she said, and moved back toward her next tour group.

In the early evening I traveled to Sperry, Oklahoma, a small town not too far from Tulsa, where the Reverend Jimmy Peters had set up his revival tent in a dust bowl hollowed out between two junkyards. The Reverend Peters moved some, the spirit or the heat moved others, while small children searched in the dust beneath the folding chairs for small change their parents might have dropped.

In the later evening, I went over to the Sperry Diner, a low slung box of a building about as flat as the Sperry countryside. When I banged the screen door of the diner, five of the six red swivel stools were occupied with enormous men dressed in sleeveless jean jackets or overalls. They wore International Harvester hats, and their wallets were chained to their belts.

I shimmied to the last stool next to a bearded man who was busy eating a hamburger bigger than his head. "Excuse me," I said, "I'm not from around these parts, but I was wondering what you thought of the fact that Oral Roberts saw a 900-foot Jesus that told him to build that hospital up the road."

While eyeing me, the man pulled flakes of hamburger from his beard. "She-it," he said.

"I beg your pardon."

"She-it. That 900-foot Jesus, I've lived in this neighborhood all my life and I ain't never seen nobody that tall."

I excused myself, walked into the bathroom, and howled like a banshee for several minutes. While in Oklahoma, all the people I had seen discussing religion had turned one syllable words into two, and two syllable words into three. Thus, Carole's say-yin had been sin; the Reverend Peters' Jey-yo-sus had been Jesus; and the truck driver had been saying shit. It is not clear whether this feature is only related to religious language or other forms of discourse as well.

. . .

The Tulsa bus station is an aging and neglected beauty: art-deco style, marble floors, a beautiful balcony with wrought-iron railings. In the center of the main concourse there are the usual plastic shell seats, this time yellow. A young Indian woman with three small children sat across the way. Child number one was a toddler with his disposable diaper hanging off the back of him. Child number two, a boy, was a three-year-old screamer. The third was an angelic-looking girl with large brown eyes and a dirty face.

To my left sat a young couple with a small girl wearing thick glasses. The child kissed the small television screen she was watching. The mother in an agitated voice gave the red-headed child a lecture on germs. The child listened dutifully and then immediately resumed kissing the screen. The mother slapped the girl hard enough to knock her off her plastic seat. I looked at the mother and said, "How would you like someone about nine feet tall to slap you like that?" The husband, a man with a dagger tattoo, looked at me and said, "How would you like to mind your own business?"

The man behind the ticket counter assured me the bus, which by then was two hours late, "will be along momentarily." The man announced the arrivals and departures in a rich baritone voice. He and his fellow worker received their pink slip yesterday. Last week Trailways was bought by Greyhound, and the Tulsa station, with its aging grace, will be one of the casualties of the merger. The nineteenth-century structure is scheduled for demolition next week.

An hour later the bus to Springfield arrived. Directly beneath the "no loitering or soliciting" sign, William asked me for "some small change to tide me over." During the wait I talked to a piano-playing Vietnam veteran who was on his way to Chicago to visit his daughter. While talking with him I became struck by how willing Americans are to share personal tragedies with strangers. He told me of his troubles with drugs, his estrangement from his wife, his inability to feel rooted in anything save the love of the little girl in Chicago. But I never learned the man's name.

. . .

We arrived in Springfield about 1:00 a.m. I slept most of the way. The driver, a tall black man without a name tag, was able to rattle off with amazing accuracy where and when our bus would go.

If bus stations are depressing during the day, they are far worse at night. When we arrived in Springfield, a man washed the marble floors with grey water that had lost its suds. I needed to get into the bathroom, but only patrons with tokens can do that. One secures a token at the ticket counter, but the ticket counter was closed. I walked outside and took a leak behind the building. This is a metaphor for the efficiency of bus travel.

. . .

Somewhere in the middle of Missouri, at 3:40 a.m. the bus brakes made that giant farting noise and four dozen lonely souls awakened to find a Mister Donut sign glowing in the window. An older black man who had been mumbling in his sleep moved off to get a donut. His hat was cocked at that impossible angle that only certain Parisians and older American black men can manage.

The donut place is next to the Nod-A-Way Motel. The blinking neon sign reflects in my window: yaW-A-doN...yaW-A-doN...yaW-A-doN. A woman across the aisle affected a deeply nasal snore, an Indian family shared one donut, the black man mumbled back on the bus.

At 5:45 our bus, which was supposed to go all the way to Chicago, came to a stop in Effingham, Illinois. We waited in Effingham, in the rain, for the Chicago bus. I asked why our original bus was not going to Chicago. The driver responded, "Well, that's because it was not the Chicago bus."

The woman who sat behind me told everyone who would listen (and those who would not) that she is sixty-five years old and has not traveled since World War II. *She* was told that *she* would not have to change buses. *She* was told that *this* bus *does* go all the way to Chicago. I told her the reason *this* bus does not go all the way to Chicago is that *it* is not the *Chicago* bus. An hour later, the Chicago bus arrived and we headed, of course, to Chicago.

We made a short rest stop in southern Illinois. I walked a few blocks looking for a *Tribune*. When I returned the man next to me lit up a cigarette. I asked him to put it out. He spent the next few minutes cursing under his breath. I asked him if he was talking to me. An hour later, I nodded off and the cursing, smoking man continued cursing and smoking.

> No I don't need a physical...(mumble, mumble, mumble)...
> I know about those sons of bitches...(mumble, mumble, mumble)...Three cheers for the mafia...

No one cheered.

An hour later, at another roadstop, we gained one female driver and lost another:

> Driver Number One: "I traded three times to get this route."
> Driver Number Two: "You going all the way to Detroit?"
> Driver Number One: "No, I'm just going to Chicago."

With this last comment, the cursing, smoking cheerer for the Mafia jumped out of his seat, ran to the front of the bus and exclaimed, "Isn't this bus going to Detroit?"

Driver Number One: "Yes, but you'll get a new driver in Chicago."

The man returned to his seat. An hour or so later, the entire bus had bedded down for a nap. The only sounds that could be heard were deviated septums and the hum of double bus tires. The calm was fractured by the cursing smoker, who sat up from a deep sleep and coarse-throated and wide-eyed scream: "No, I don't know a psychiatry professor at Duke University."

An hour later we arrived in Chicago. The cursing smoker who I thought was continuing on to Detroit, exited the bus. As he came to the threshold of the steps he looked back in what I took to be my direction, and once again screamed, "Go to the monastery and pray for your soul. That's what I'd do. I'd become a monk."

. . .

An hour later our bus left for Detroit. Across the way a man with a muscle shirt and handlebar mustache debated a number of issues in animal rights with a young woman whom fate had placed beside him. They eventually arrived at the question of whether fish can scream. He was in favor of the proposition. She remained skeptical through much of Illinois and a good bit of Michigan.

The Detroit station has one of those wooden holding pens in its center. A bank of twelve television sets lined one wall. They were black sets attached to black shell seats. The scene looked like a bunch of unlikely people turned into some strange stationary motorcycle gang.

On the other three walls were the usual yellow shell seats. I sat at the far end of the enclosure and watched a mother and her two children eat enormous hoagies. (You may want to substitute the word "grinder" or "submarine" to finish the last sentence. One thing I did learn this summer on the bus is that the same sandwich is known by at least five different names throughout the country.) The mother talked to her children about moving all their belongings from Cincinnati to northern Texas.

A black woman with cornrows sat all the way to the other end of the enclosure. Her son, about six, played with his Masters of the Universe dolls, who mostly slammed into each other with great force. The boy supplied the crashing sound effects.

Next to me the hoagie mother went to check on her luggage. This was a cue for her children to make throwing-up noises at each other. The black woman at the other end began talking to a man with a bandana who looked like Willy Nelson. Tattooed on his arm was a pale blue snake that ran the length of his forearm. The woman's son had moved to the turnstile which he spun over and over again. The hoagie mother returned with what at first looked like a can of tennis balls. A moment later three hoagie eaters were sharing potato chips.

A few moments later the two hoagie children moved to the television sets. They dropped a quarter in one of the machines and tuned in "The Price is Right." Bob Barker's disembodied assistant was telling Eileen Leeks to "come on down." The little boy continued to make throwing-up noises. Bob told us he had three winners in a row. The children changed the channel. A narrator in the Crayola Crayon advertisement gravely explained, "The child who creates is the child who prospers." The little boy had begun to create burping noises. There was an announcement for a bus to Pittsburgh. I moved to the Pittsburgh line where I stood for an hour.

While in line I met Edna and Velma, two sisters in their eighties who were traveling to Pittsburgh to visit Edna's daughter. During the wait we discussed buses, books, politics, and grandchildren. These were two of the most delightful people on the trip.

The bus to Pittsburgh was the cleanest of all I had taken: overhead luggage compartments with doors, beautiful multi-colored velour seats. The driver made his usual announcements, adding that we would be in Pittsburgh two hours late.

Driver: "We are in a period of transition. On behalf of Greyhound/Trailways, I want to thank you for your patience. Praise the Lord."

In Cambridge, Ohio, a woman exited the bus. A few moments earlier she had been telling the bus driver (whom she had correctly identified as a "Christian") about her daughter the prostitute. The woman was replaced by a small woman who looked and walked like a charter member of the Lollypop League. The driver and the new woman began to discuss the grace of God. The driver now spoke in the plural.

Driver: "And we think of that man in Rome, Italy, who missed the transport plane, and that plane went down, and all the men on that plane died. We think about that man. That was the grace of God."

From somewhere behind me a New York accent piped up, "I think about the guys who died."

. . .

The houses in western Pennsylvania dot the Allegheny Mountains like a Greek postcard. By 4:45 p.m. we arrived in Washington, Pennsylvania. The Gibson Photo Company, across from the train station, featured a huge camera with blinking flash attachment that hung on the side of the building. Next to the photo shop was an exterminating company, The Pest Doctors. Their sign read: "All Our Patients Die." The born-again driver and an old man with an eastern European accent talked about jobs they have had. The driver spoke in the plural about working in a slaughterhouse. The old man spoke of delivering newspapers in the '20s for forty cents a week. The strata on the rock that lines this highway in western Pennsylvania look like the ridges in conch shells.

We arrived in Pittsburgh at 5:45 p.m. I headed for the Weston Willian Penn.

* * *

    I arrived back at the Pittsburgh station at 11:00 the following morning. Five Amish teenagers waited patiently as a sixth sought information about bus routes. The three girls wore black bonnets and long cotton dresses with black tie shoes like those worn by the nuns in my Catholic grade school in the 1950s. The boys wore light blue work shirts with the sleeves rolled up, dark blue pants, and the male version of the black shoes. The six stole glances around the station at what to them must have seemed an extraordinary collection of human beings: a 300-pound security guard with a billy club; a fifteen-year-old man/child with shoulder length hair and a tattoo which proclaimed "Born to Lose" above a large red and blue snake on his skinny right arm; a large black man with a shaved head. He wore purple trousers and matching purple shoes. They all stared at the Amish. The Amish furtively stared back.

* * *

    Somewhere outside of Breezewood, on Route 30, the driver stopped the bus. He walked back to the rear to tell two elderly men to put away their whiskey bottle. The bends and dips of Route 30 remind one of a roller coaster ride. I tried to imagine drinking whiskey under those conditions.
    We arrived in Breezewood, "the town of motels," at 2:10. The muzak in the men's room was playing "Born Free." My last bus was a Trailways to Baltimore. I spent the two-hour wait talking to Greyhound drivers seated by the video games. A tall thin driver put his quarter in the machine, a game that simulated the movement of a high speed race car, and crashed a moment later. The bus driver continued to feed quarters into the machine, and continued to crash. Several other Greyhound employees talked about incorporating the Trailways drivers into their company. None were very optimistic.

At 4:10 I boarded the Trailways bus for Baltimore. It was the only bus of the eighty-three departures and arrivals that was on time.

The trees outside Frederick were tall and straight. Clouds piled on the horizons. They looked like the tops of vanilla ice cream cones. The faint small of marijuana wafted through the bus. The driver, a powerfully built man with reflective sun glasses, made an announcement over the intercom: "Whoever is smoking that stuff in the back of my bus better just put that away right now, 'cause I can just as easily make an unscheduled stop at the police station right over here in Frederick."

One of the old men who had his whiskey bottle taken away earlier gave out with a raspy "Oh Daddy" when he read the green and white highway sign for Baltimore County.

The bus pulled up to the Trailways terminal on Fayette Street in Baltimore. As the bus made its wide turn I could see a one-legged man with crutches who had rested his stump on the top of a white lattice-work trash can. On the side of the can was an orange and black sign done in a basketball motif. The sign read: "Jump One In."

The bus station looked like a bus station: dirty linoleum covering the floor, orange seats, hustlers, street people, lonely travelers, some going home, but most going nowhere. I exited through the Fayette Street side of the building. I was met on the street by a cab driver with a leather hat and eyes like picked clean watermelon rinds.

"Do you want a taxi, mister?"

"No, thank you," I said. "I think I'll take the bus."

*July-August, 1987*

# Love

*A man is shaped and fashioned by what he loves.*
　　　　　—GOETHE

# Not Writing about My Mother

I have never written about my mother. Let me amend that. I have never published anything about her.

I have tried to say about her what I now realize must remain unsaid. The attempts always look like the day's production of a failed poet writing copy for a greeting card company. I don't want to embarrass myself as a writer, or, I guess, as a man, so I have published nothing about the woman who gave me birth.

In a letter written in 1936, D.H. Lawrence remarked, "Nobody can have the soul of me. My mother has had it, and nobody can have it again. Nobody can come into my very self again, and breathe me like an atmosphere." Most sons know something of these sentiments, but these days a man risks embarrassment or the threat of instant psychoanalysis at the expression of them.

My father has always been much easier. He is the subject of a number of my essays and stories. Usually he appears pretty much looking like himself; sometimes I give him a Groucho nose and glasses. Only outsiders wonder who he might be.

But writing about my mother is different. There can be no artifice. She is too much a part of who and what I have become. This is why I have not written about her.

A few weeks ago, the mother of a good friend died after waging a determined battle with cancer. The woman and her family had only known of the disease for a short time. Death sat silently coiled inside her small frame. She decided on aggressive treatment, but the intruder would not leave its hiding place. A few days after the completion of her first round of chemotherapy and radiation, my friend's mother died.

When I saw my friend a few days later, she looked the same as always—except her eyes. They were like a raccoon's, ringed black for mourning. On the inside, where we all live and love and remember, the change was much greater. I knew if somehow I could peer through those black-ringed eyes to the very insides of my friend, I would see that she had begun a terrible free-fall.

That is what death of a mother must do to a child, no matter what the child's age. Every adult carries with her the child she once was. The sense of smallness forms a substratum of the mind. Ineradicably, one's triumphs are measured against this smallness; the loss of one's mother substantiates it. And this is what so often begins the secret free-fall.

The death of my friend's mother has called to mind that my family was once given a reprieve. A few years ago, my mother became very ill. I thought about how much she looked like the women in those photographs from the death camps. I thought about all those mothers, and about their children free-falling. I could not write about my mother, not even then. Longfellow tells us, "There is no grief like the grief that does not speak."

But my mother did not die. She recovered miraculously, and I was saved from that yawning hole my friend avoids during the day but falls into at night.

Someday I will say about my mother what needs to be said. But she will be gone and my words will be written, not in embarrassment, but in sorrow. I wish I could say them now, while I am watching my friend fall.

I wish my mother could know before it's too late.

*November, 1988*

# Talking to Myself

There is a Henry James novel going on in the hollow of my head. Each of the characters is some part of my collective self; many of them speak in subordinate clauses or lengthy run-on sentences with little or no punctuation. The whole experience is something like having an overactive high school debating society living permanently in my skull.

I cannot remember when I first began talking to myself in earnest. I suspect it was quite early on. By now, however, the cast of characters is quite impressive, even if I do say so myself. There is a radio sports announcer who has taken up permanent residence. He regularly broadcasts my major athletic accomplishments, both real and imagined.

Then there is a man who has been directing a play in the middle of my head for years. Of course, I play the leading role and I sit in all the seats, filling the audience to standing room only. The drama has had an enormously long and successful run. It has enjoyed wonderfully enthusiastic reviews, which I have skillfully written.

There is also a man who talks to me in the morning. I usually meet him at the mirror when I am shaving. Frequently, he is bored with my baloney. He thinks the only reason I write, or fall in love, is to confess to others what earlier I had a difficult time selling to myself.

I suspect we all have these various voices. This is perhaps one of the surest differences between ourselves and the other animals—one of the incontrovertible signs that we are as human as possible. It is almost as if what it means to be a person is to have the capacity to be a whole crowd of persons, and it is in our being part of the crowd,

I think, that art emerges. Rhetoric, it is sometimes said, is what may be made out of the quarrels with others. But it is poetry that comes from disagreements with ourselves. Surely this is one of the more profound things we learn from Hamlet. The stage is filled with only Hamlet and a series of tragic cartoon balloons that drift eerily above his head.

"I have done that," says my memory. "I could not have done that," intones my pride. They wrestle in the evening, like Jacob and the angel of God, until by first light pride has yielded. It is in the hollow of my head, and usually in the dead of night, where I regularly bear witness against myself. The drama in my head has had more than enough court scenes. I am jury, judge and all the witnesses. I am usually found guilty. But it is only then, as in Kafka, that the drama has the possibility to become art.

I have only lately begun to realize, as I think Kafka never did, that despite the many voices in my head, there is an important one missing. The vanished voice is the one that might treat myself with the graciousness I reserve for others. There is profound irony in looking at the withdrawn face of another and always crediting him with a mystery and profundity I cannot reserve for myself.

It is with perfect strangers I am usually so willing to forgive. But I know my own faults in the minutest of details. It is this voice of forgiveness I cannot find. It is a voice with subtlety and depth, a voice with a power whose echo cannot be found in the chartered regions of myself.

And yet I know if in the past I have forgiven others I must first have possessed forgiveness in an undiscovered province of myself. But these days there are no maps available for that place. And so, in the meantime, I live with a curious hope shared by all the voices. It is a hope that some day, this forgiving voice may surge up out of the depth of my being from a forgotten country, from a still place where God used to speak.

*June, 1987*

# The Uses of Tears

> *Did he break into tears?... a kind of overflow of kindness: there is no face truer than those so washed.*
> —William Shakespeare, *Much Ado About Nothing*

For the past few minutes I have been thinking about tears. A student left a few moments ago, leaving some tears behind. Some of the drops fell on the carpet of my office floor. After she left, I walked to the spot and placed my fingers where the drops had landed. The carpet was still wet.

The student told a story that goes well beyond the usual sophomore worries. It was a tale about grief and pain, a story about loss of friendship and early death, and the courage that must rise up to meet these experiences. As the tale unfolded, I could feel myself wanting to cry.

In her own way, the student had asked me about the human condition, the same questions asked by the philosophers she had studied with me in class: why do the innocent suffer? What meaning can we ascribe to the experience of intense and unremitting pain? In my own way, I tried to tell her that pain and suffering are not just symptoms that could be removed without changing life. They are, rather, the fullest mode, along with joy, in which life is expressed.

As our conversation progressed, it was clear that this was the first time she fully understood the tragic discord between imagination and fact. When she left my office, she entered a world that to her mind had undergone a dramatic and irrevocable transformation. It was not just that a few more leaves had pulled their life-stems from mother trees on this overcast fall day. It was that the looking at trees and leaves, or anything else of genuine importance in life, would never be the same.

Many tears I see shed by sophomores are used as weapons: against me, against their parents, against the expectations of their families. They sometimes rail at their teachers or the institution because they cannot become what they are told they must become. They see themselves as failures, and then they cry. It is the kind of emotion displayed because of too little planning and too much play. The tears come as a plea or a last act of contrition before the semester's fate is sealed and sent off to their waiting parents.

But the student who just left is different. She talked about her parents wishing to keep the truth from her about the prognosis of a dying friend. They wanted to save their daughter from the tears. Her mother and father made that act of the will that good parents often do to eliminate from their daughter's field of vision all that might remind her too quickly of the mystery and sorrow of adulthood.

But these wishes of parents always fail, as the tale of the Buddha's three passing sights reminds us that they must. In the failure the student saw something clearly for the first time—that tears are not always marks of weakness but of a special kind of strength, a power to feel more completely human than the rest.

I learned of this particular power one evening several years ago. I sat in a hospital room where my mother lay waiting for a miracle which later would save her life. My father stood by the rain-streaked window. As drops moved silently down the pane, tears welled up in his blue eyes. As if by sympathetic magic, they ran like tiny rivers down the sides of his weathered face. I had not seen my father cry in the thirty years before, nor in the eight years since. I saw in him that night a special kind of strength, a power to feel more humanly than I thought was possible for him.

In my office, the student learned something of that power. She understood the difference between a legal contrition, one usually experienced after the fact, and a deeper kind, one that assumes blame even without guilt. It is only in the latter, of course, that tears act as messengers of overwhelming grief and unspeakable love. And it is these tears that eventually allow the heart to breathe more freely.

She understood, I think, that a tearless grief bleeds inwardly. It is like a secret hemorrhage that must kill something healthy inside in order to ease the pain.

Before she left, I wanted to hug the woman, and I wanted to cry—for her, for her dying friend, for all who have felt this sublime pain. But more than this, I wanted to tell her something my father taught me eight years ago in a darkened room: that if there is a God, He had decided it was only to tears He would give the awesome responsibility of doing what sometimes even the best of words cannot. And then I wanted to cry with her.

*November, 1988*

# Death of a Drugstore

The Irvington Pharmacy is dead. It gave up the ghost sometime last month. It's always such a tricky matter pinpointing the exact time of death and all the more difficult when the dearly departed is a drugstore. What we do know is that T.S. Eliot was right about this one: It went not with a bang, but with a whimper.

I was informed of the store's passing by a neatly lettered black and yellow sign posted at the entrance. I had gone to have a prescription refilled, so the death came as a surprise. It always seems easier when there is a little anticipatory grief, a bit of lead time to get used to the idea of the finite, but it didn't happen that way with the drugstore's demise.

The sign told me to have my prescription refilled at the Rite-Aid, where, when I went to pay by check, I needed "three pieces of valid identification." When I paid by check at the Irvington Pharmacy, my identity was always verified by benign, blue-haired ladies who squinted over the counter to see if I looked like one of Mrs. Vicchio's boys. I thought about this when I left the Rite-Aid. That's when it became clear the pharmacy was dead.

For over forty years the owner, Tim Cragg, opened his store for business, seven days a week, through forty flu seasons, the hayfevers of many springs, through summers of sunburns and the selling of four decades of back-to-school supplies. Sometime last month, the kindly pharmacist performed drugstore euthanasia. He pulled the plug before the old pharmacy did itself in.

When I was a small child there was a penny scale in front. You got not only your weight but a line or two about your future. But that was when the store windows displayed apothecary jars and wonderfully exotic glass bottles filled with mysterious crimson-colored liquids. Back then the pharmacy had a soda fountain, whose red plastic and chrome swivel stools were presided over by the omni-present and efficient "Miss Mary." One of her many jobs was to escort Straty, the community crazy person, out through the thick glass double doors whenever he came near the *bona fide* customers.

The pharmacy held a central place in my early life. It was halfway between home and the Catholic school four blocks to the east. It also became a place to hide on Sunday mornings. While classmates were doing hard time with the principle parts of the Mass, I was sipping cherry Coke and talking about the June Taylor dancers I had seen the evening before on the Jackie Gleason show. On Sunday morning we called the drugstore "Our Lady of Rexall," and Miss Mary was our unwitting patron saint.

I noticed last evening that dirt and candy wrappers already have found their way to the corners of the store's worn marble steps. The vertical sign announcing "Pharmacy" was cold and dark. The ugly orange and blue Rexall signs could hardly be seen.

Over the years the outside of the building came to look like the dressing habits of a man with multiple personalities. There was the Victorian roof with A-frame propriety; then came the art-deco facade, all chrome and straight-lined glass. The final layer was a 1970s recession makeover; big display windows on one side were replaced by ugly and impenetrable blue plastic.

As the exterior changed, so did the neighborhood. There were the original Irvington families, old money, wrap-around porches and widow's walks. They were followed by the poor of all colors and finally, yuppies looking for good buys.

In recent years, the inside of the pharmacy also changed. The soda fountain was removed; Straty was buried among the granite angels of Loudon Park Cemetery. Most recently, the display window was filled with prosthetic devices; cough syrup and hypodermic syringes were kept behind the counter. Turnstiles were placed at the entrance and plexiglass was installed to separate customers from employees. Lines formed at the new lottery machine.

All of this, and the holdups and the burglaries and the shoplifting made Dr. Tim pull the plug. It must have been difficult. He had sent his daughter to pharmacy school.

Most likely I will not see the quiet and kind Cragg again—that gentle man with the starched white pharmacy coat. Nor will I see his wife, a woman with eyes of the same blue as the stained-glass windows of the monastery a few blocks away. And I'm sure Forrest, the young assistant pharmacist who came out from behind the counter to talk to his customers, is now no more than a part of the past.

The memory of the pharmacy and its people will be put away with the other pebbles retrieved from life's shores. I do not doubt the most important things are always the best remembered, for it seems recollection is the only paradise from which we are never entirely evicted.

And if by some chance, either here or in some other life, the folks at the pharmacy were to reappear, I would thank them for caring about my family all those years.

*February, 1989*

# The Cloud Velocity Detection Position

> *Bright towers of silence,
> stiff sculpted like a
> heap of marble flowers.*
> —Edward Shanks, "Clouds"

Very early in life I came to learn that the speed of clouds is best measured from a position parallel to, and in firm contact with, the ground. This afternoon, while wondering with my family in a Homewood sculpture garden, we assumed the cloud velocity detection position—the bodies of two thirtysomethings and a four year old splayed beneath pieces of iron and sculpted stone bearing names like "Large Boxing Hare on Anvil."

Overhead, above the swaying oval window made by the tops of towering trees, a group of white clouds, looking as intricate as a map of the Greek isles, slowly drifted east in the direction of an invisible Asia Minor.

When one is upright and walking around, it is not so easy to mark the movement of the clouds. When they are noticed, it is usually with a utilitarian interest, for what they may or may not bring. But in the cloud velocity detection position, the interest becomes aesthetic, the simplest changes become readily apparent, a series of small reports of a great and ephemeral work in progress.

I learned this little trick about the speed of clouds—and perhaps the velocity of our individual lives—from an uncle with whom I stretched out on the grass in the tiny yard of my grandmother's row house sometime in the Fall of 1956. My grandfather, my uncle's father, had died suddenly a few days before. The ground was wet and grief mixed with curiosity as we lay in the middle of the yard trying to understand one of nature's hieroglyphs.

In the years since that day, I saw my uncle only on rare occasions. He died earlier this month of a heart ailment bequeathed him by my bookish grandfather. From what I know of my uncle, he lived a life of accomplishment, but one where the velocity of clouds still played more than a minor role.

Before he died, he left word with his wife that he wished me to speak to their twenty-year-old son about "some important things in life." I don't know for sure what my uncle had in mind, but he made his request from a hospital bed, as close as he could be to the cloud velocity detection position.

For two weeks now, I have been trying to compose a letter to my young cousin. This afternoon, while looking at the slow movement of the clouds and the first of fragile leaves disconnected and fluttering to an early end, I want to tell him something about how we are all as ephemeral as the clouds, so we must watch carefully for the beautiful. I want to mention how his father taught me as a frightened, grieving child that few adults can really see nature, and about how sometimes life must be slowed to a snail's speed, where real seeing is possible.

Toward the end of his life, Thoreau remarked in his journal that the ancients, with their centaurs and sphinxes, could imagine far more than exists. We moderns have an increasingly difficult time just imagining the natural.

In this early autumnal quiet, I am searching among the leaves and in those first breaths of cold air for something to tell my cousin about his grief, something that Keats understood by looking at an urn. That day in 1956 my uncle tried to tell me that beauty usually comes in small, nearly imperceptible moments—that traveling at the wrong speed is the surest way to miss most of them.

What is clear, even thirty-four years later, is that my uncle had a real inkling of the sadness that comes when even the smallest of opportunities is missed. As much as accomplishments, a completed life is a catalogue of what one has slowed down to see. When it comes to clouds, the best way to do it is by first assuming the cloud velocity detection position.

*October, 1990*

# Sappho and the Bittersweet

The delight that comes with love, the kind filled with passion, and the mystery of how that delight is so easily lost, has exercised my imagination since I first took notice of girls sometime during the first day of fifth grade.

School began that September as usual: textbooks jacketed in makeshift brown paper covers; number two pencils sharpened to the finest of points; stiff blue duffel bags with white pullcords slung over our shoulders. But this year was different. It brought us Deborah, a willowy girl with chestnut colored hair whose parental break-up had bestowed fortune on those with budding testosterone in Mrs. Frey's class. By recess that first day, Deborah had sent shivers up the spines of every child wearing a starched white shirt and blue clip-on tie in room 5A.

It took but a few days for the bloom to fall from the rose. Deborah was more interested in boys who fell under the general category of the tall and the smart than she was in me. This did not make the passion dim, but the longing did, after a short while, begin to mix itself with something else—a special kind of disappointment that later in life, after too many like experiences, might easily be mislabeled "bitterness."

It was Sappho, the seventh-century B.C. poet and iconoclast who is acknowledged as first suggesting that eros is bittersweet. But in translation the fullness of her insight is nearly lost, for in the Greek the compound *glukupikron* is "sweetbitter," as if the poet were trying to tell us something important about the chronology of eros. It is not just in ancient verse that love ends so badly. Freud suggests in his *Civilization and Its Discontents* that we are never so defenseless against suffering as when we love, never so forlornly unhappy as when we have lost that love.

Young love so often seems to make of itself a gossamer web. The points it clings to—the things that connect its intricate interlacings—are scarcely perceptible, and yet, are counted as the most real, the most delightful: momentary touches of fingertips, a faint tremor brought by a single glance, a cheek faintly brushed but brought to fever because of it, a vow of love expressed in the dark like millions of lovers who have come before, a yearning of one life toward another.

And yet, the longing after these threads, long after they are gone, is an object lesson in the brilliance of Sappho's philology. In eros, disappointments so often track the steps of hope, never really obliterating them but retracing them in reverse, like a lost man caught in a deep snowfall.

In a poem the British poet Philip Larkin calls "Two Portraits of Sex," he brings Sappho's observation into English. After describing a woman lost to him, not dead, but lost *to* him, he writes:

> No one can migrate across your boundaries.
> No one can exist without a habit for you.
> No one can tear your thread out of himself.
> No one can tie you down or set you free.
> Apart from your tribe, there is only the dead.

Now, after too many loves where one or the other has fanned the bright flame of passion into a raging blaze, I wonder too much about *glukupikron*. I wonder, perhaps after a certain Archimedian point, if the lover's world cannot be put back on its original orbit.

If there is any salvation to be sought or found in the experience of love and its loss, it is, perhaps, to be found in the making of art, where all sorrow, all bitterness must finally be lifted, if not forever, at least for the moment.

But what of those denied Sappho's muse, those without Larkin's alchemical ability to turn blood to ink? What are they to do with *glukupikron*? The Scots have a proverb that "Love is like a cough, it cannot be hid." But perhaps it is more like a cough because we have such difficulty in making it go away.

*November, 1989*

# Dancing with My Sisters

Self-confidence may be the most elusive and ephemeral of human gifts. For those who have it, self-possession floats on the surface of a life like a thin film of dark oil atop a deep sea, keeping things from breaking the surface. I began thinking about self-confidence and self-consciousness while musing aloud with a female friend about my social behavior as a fourteen-year-old boy.

These were the years of CYO (Catholic Youth Organization) dances, where I would stand with other likeminded fourteen- and fifteen-year-old boys, close to the wall, as if unconsciously hankering for protection from something, while out in the middle of the dance floor the girls were busy bopping, twisting, jitter-bugging, and generally having a good time.

We boys stood rigidly, arms folded, feet riveted to the floor, while the girls giggled and glided, seeming to pay us little if any attention.

I do not know much of the home lives of those other adolescent boys, but there was something curious about my time at home that did not quite match my behavior at the dances.

At home, atop the oval hooked rug and in front of the cathode ray image of Buddy Deane that flickered across the Muntz, my sisters had taught me to dance. The twins, a year older and many years wiser, out of the goodness of their hearts or possibly the need for a partner with a little testosterone, had initiated me into the mysteries of the bop and the slow dance.

Three or four afternoons a week we would glide, stomp, and twirl until Buddy gave way to Rocky and

Bullwinkle. Each week, while dancing with my sisters, I secretly vowed that next Friday I would not spend the evening holding in place my portion of the school wall's plaster. When the weekend rolled around, however, the good times did not roll with it. I always assumed my place amidst the wall liners whose conversation inevitably turned to how there weren't any girls worth dancing with anyway. The truth of the matter, of course, was not so simple. In those skinny human frames dabbed with too much English Leather, the fear of ridicule had somehow married the most delicate kind of machismo to produce a predictable inaction—an inaction born in early adolescence and not so easily lost. There was a simple human law at work among the wall liners: doing nothing can produce no pain; nothing ventured, nothing lost.

Now, a quarter of a century later, I try to look back at that boy as if he were another person. I try to convince myself that because I don't stand around at CYO dances helping to hold the walls in place, that I somehow have managed to find that thin film of self-possession that might ride a personal sea, which so often has been without easily discernible harbors.

The truth of the matter is that I am the same boy with a few more wrinkles and many more scars—and many of those, I fear, have been self-inflicted.

We are such a curious species, *homo sapiens*, so much rooted in what cannot be seen, so haunted by what is too much felt. There is a scintilla of the fourteen-year-old in every catch of the throat, in every longer look in the mirror. And by their collective force these small reminders of vulnerability must convince me of the difficulty in finding that layer of self-confidence, and how simple it is, in the turning of the tide, to disperse it.

By adulthood most of us pretend that we need not rely on others for the making of that layer of confidence. It is in the making of the protest that the lie pops from beneath the surface, ready to expose us as surely as a man who tries to speak an unknown tongue to the natives.

There are events in each of our lives—a Friday evening at a school dance—that act as small drops colliding against a giant stone of the self. After a while the drops make their mark. After a while the drops become the stone.

*December, 1989*

# The Old Neighborhood

I don't walk through my old neighborhood much anymore, although I still live just on the edge of it. I always drive through, usually preoccupied with where I have to be rather than with what has happened to these three blocks of storefronts in west Baltimore.

This neighborhood is a part of the past, removed yet unspeakably near. There was, in the beginning, an image. Now what is left is composite, stranger and yet more real than the image itself. Like most afterimages, it is a disturbing spectre—the picture of a neighborhood on its deathbed. It is a neighborhood dying, dying of a thousand disappointments.

Buildings in a fading community always seem so much like the people who live in them: old and bent, gravity and circumstance playing terrible tricks on skin and bone, brick and mortar. The weathered facades only hint at the devastation which lies within.

Gone is the penny candy store presided over by the exquisitely rotund Miss Leidig whose loose alabaster skin sagged beneath her abundant upper arms. When she gave children change, the skin swayed to and fro like a happy man on a lazy hammock.

Gone, too, is the burned-down bowling alley. It was brought down to its foundations by fire when I was learning to walk. Through my childhood the rubble-filled lot remained untouched; a few charred timbers still stood in the rear of the property when I graduated from high school.

In recent years, the bowling alley lot was paved over to make room for a parking lot full of cars as dilapidated as the buildings between which they sit.

The neighborhood bars, the Half-Mile Track and the Kozy Klub, are still in business. But the red and black swivel stools that line their bars stay occupied for most of the workday by men out of work.

Frank's Shoe Repair is still a few shops away. Thirty years ago the proprietor's son and namesake sat ostracized in my third-grade class. He was guilty of possession of dark stained fingernails acquired polishing shoes in his father's shop.

Loudon Park Cemetery still serves as a kind of *axis mundi* for the community. It is one of the only places in the neighborhood where property values have not gone down. It is in the graveyard's dark brown earth that most of the community's inhabitants will one day find a resting place while they wait for the resurrection. The old people who still sit on their porches on warm summer nights hope the Second Coming will bring a better life than this one.

The massive stone monastery across from the cemetery will soon be sold to the owner of a chain of nursing homes. The entrepreneur has plans to make it a drug rehabilitation center. The ironies are too many and too painful to enumerate, so the neighborhood's residents translate the hurt into a split community association vote, about whether it would be better to welcome the businessman or simply have the monastery lay fallow until some religious order becomes interested in saving the community's soul.

Next to the monastery there now stands a combination twenty-four-hour convenience store and self-serve gas station. It costs twenty-five cents to fill one's tires with air. Back when air was free, that same corner was home to a noble filling station with grease monkeys who pulled faded red rags from the back pockets of their work-stained overalls to see what the trouble was under the hood.

At the entrance to the old gas station sat an enormous yellow-gold cowrie shell atop a great thirty-foot pole. The red letters across the golden fan of a shell stated the obvious.

Among the ancient Egyptians the cowrie shell was a sign of immortality.

*July, 1987*

# Scattered Pieces

*Life, like a dome of many-colored glass,
stains white radiance of eternity.*
—SHELLEY

# Baseball:
# Spring's First Great Conviction

*All winter long I am one for whom the bell is tolling;*
*I can arouse no interest in basketball,*
*indoor, fly-casting or bowling;*
*The sports pages are strictly no soap,*
*and until they cry* Play Ball! *I simply mope.*
—Ogden Nash

In late winter my thoughts seem to travel like the shadows made when walking away from the morning sun. The thoughts, like shadows, slightly precede me; they are just a little larger than myself. This morning those thoughts have turned to baseball.

Winter is such a difficult time. Things are cold and dead. Clouds pile up in the sky like heaps of white marble flowers. Their cold scent burns the nostrils. The only games to watch are football and basketball, two sports too much bounded by space and time.

The ancient Greeks, a people very good at games, had two words for time, *kronos* and *kairos*. The first was clock time, sundial time, time measured out in small, equally divisible increments. It is time that reminds us, like winter, of death. The other notion of time, *kairos,* was the "right" time, an auspicious time, and time that suggested miracle and serendipity are not always so easily distinguished.

Time in baseball is *kairos*, not *kronos*. Unlike basketball and football, games which live and die at the hands of the clock, baseball's time, as Roger Angell reminded us, "ticks inwardly and silently." It can be as short as a two-hour pitchers' duel or as interminable as a rain delay. Lurking in the background of every baseball game is that very strange metaphysical possibility that the first batter will foul off pitches from now until the end of time. Time at the ball park is not measured in halves and quarters; it is parceled out in hits and runs, plays at the plate and foul tips on a three-and-two count.

Football and basketball are played by giants for the amusement of lilliputians. Baseball is played and watched by people who look like the guy next door. With little difficulty, you can convince yourself, if not others, that the only difference between you and the players is that they hit the curve ball a little better.

Football by its very nature involves one in violence and suffering. As spectators it sometimes imprisons us in the worst kind of voyeurism, a gratuitously violent kind. Football forces us to think about death. Baseball allows us, at least for a while, to exclude the necessity of time, of suffering and of death.

The game we call our national pastime, like the country itself, is bound up in enormous paradoxes. It is a sport where the foul lines are fair, where a hit-and-run is a run-and-hit, and where Casey Stengel, one of the great managers of the game, could regularly utter sentences like, "They say you can't do it, but sometimes it doesn't always work."

Baseball is a game where reality is routinely suspended until rotund men in blue bark out their less than omniscient versions of space. As former umpire Bill Klem puts it, "It ain't nothin' till I call it." The instant replay is something used by fans, not umpires.

Space in the summer games is not what Newton had in mind. It is measured out in nearly imperceptible little nervous half-steps with which infielders accompany each pitch. It is a strike zone that moves according to Einstein, not Newton. It grows, moves left and right, up and down, according to who is pitching and who is hitting (and who is umpiring). It is a game where sometimes the most important space in the park is the cheap seats where a home run has just been hit.

Unlike other sports, baseball has no college apprenticeship. Baseball players are usually much more honest about whether they are really students or not. Minor league baseball is the life of a poor intern, the cloistered seminarian, a traveling salesman on a small expense account. It is dimly lit parks, cold food and bus rides between places left behind by *kronos*. In the minor leagues, as in religion, one trusts a reward will be found in the future. But in baseball, it is never a salvation by grace; it is always a salvation by works.

Baseball is a game where the fans, often quite rightly, think they know more about the game than the people who get paid to manage and coach it. It is a sport with a magic, almost Pythagorean, respect for numbers. As Arthur Daley puts it, "The baseball fan has the digestive tract of a billy goat." He can, and usually does, devour the most disparate collection of statistics, folklore and hotdogs from a silver box.

Emily Dickenson once wrote that the crocus is spring's first great conviction. She was wrong. It is baseball—a game that ushers in life and banishes death, a sport that trades *kronos* for *kairos*.

Roger Kahn, in *The Second Fireside Book of Baseball,* warns that the romance between intellectuals and the game of baseball is, for the most part, one-sided.

Ah, unrequited love is always so much better in the spring.

*March, 1986*

# Talking to Dogs

I have come to notice in the past few years that talking to dogs has reached a degree and frequency heretofore unknown to *homo sapiens,* or even to *canis familiaris,* the family dog. I was reminded of this fact the other day while sitting in the park adjacent to the Washington Monument on Charles Street.

A large elderly woman dressed in a long cloth coat walked a bow-legged boxer past the bench on which two street people and I were spending the noon hour. The dog was dressed in a green knit sweater.

As he sniffed around the edge of the dry, lifeless fountain at the center of the park, the woman's attention remained fixed on the dog. Her face was like that of an aged Raggedy Ann doll—large circles of scarlet provided the color for both cheeks. After a few moments, she spoke in the general direction of the dog who was busy with natural matters. "Hurry up, Sweetie," she said, "we don't want to miss the man from the drycleaners."

As woman and dog headed out of the park, the other occupants of my bench looked at each other with that smile which only comes when two people are thinking precisely the same thought. The younger man, with hair the color of a rusted saw, squinted at the receding figures. "And they say street people is crazy," he said.

Now my scientist friends tell me the dog is one of the oldest of domesticated animals. He has been a member of the human household for millennia. In the evolutionary time before domestication, *canis familiaris* was much larger and ferocious, looking more like a wolf than a shitzu. *Homo sapiens,* of course, was also much more aggressive and blood-thirsty at the time, and his vocabulary was not so nearly well developed. As the brain of *homo sapiens* grew, he was, by degrees, capable of formulating concepts as complex as "hurry up," "sweetie," and "drycleaning man." *Canis familiaris,* in order to avoid extinction, and to keep its preferred place in the domesticated hierarchy, had to follow suit.

Still, there is in the woman's behavior something akin to what Kierkegaard would call a "leap of faith." The street people viewed her remark as an absurd comment hurled in the general direction of the Great Void, something about which street people know a great deal. These two men were incapable of the woman's brand of faith, at least with respect to the dog. I am not sure where I stand on the general issue of dog consciousness.

Later in the day, while sitting in a committee meeting, I began smiling secretly, the kind of grin produced when no other human being could possibly be having the same thought as mine. The thought was that somewhere in Baltimore a little man was driving around in a white drycleaning truck. Behind his seat, hanging on a metal pole which stretched the width of the truck, are a group of small, neatly pressed, green sweaters wrapped in the kind of glossy plastic bags in which small children are not supposed to place their heads. I'm sure the lady has explained to her boxer the dangers of those plastic bags. But there are two street people in a park on Charles Street who would not be convinced the dog understood.

*March, 1987*

# Pictures from the Radio

I recall the day my father brought home our first television set. From the front, it looked as if an enormous imitation walnut box somehow had swallowed a tiny seven-inch screen. A large piece of stiff perforated cardboard covered the back. When one peered through the hundreds of little round holes, the insides of the set looked like the metropolitan area of Oz seen at night—glowing tubes of various sizes stood side by side like a model of some enormous and complicated city of the future.

After various members of my extended family nearly went blind squinting at the seven-inch Admiral, my parents, a few years later, decided Jack Parr might look a little better if he weren't so small. My father went out and bought a Muntz. It took two strong men to get it in the house. The picture was large enough for my sisters and me to draw on something called a Winky Dink Screen, a sort of neolithic experiment in reactive television.

On Saturdays we watched Film Funnies, Hop-A-Long Cassidy, and Sky King. Roy and Dale came on later in the afternoon just before the weekly supply of accordion players and tap dancers squeezed and tapped across the stage of Ted Mack's Amateur Hour. During the week we received regular doses of Miss Nancy's Romper Room, Captain Kangaroo, and when we were allowed to stay up, the Texaco Star Theatre and the evening variety shows. When these programs came on the air, our house was like pictures I have seen of small contemporary Chinese villages. We had the only TV in the neighborhood. People crowded into the house to watch ventriloquists and dog acts. Grown men with long legs and white socks stretched out on our living room floor like refugees from a vanishing radio era.

Gabby Hayes was the spokesman for Twenty Mule Team Borax. He may have been the last person without a tooth in his head to sell anything on television. Later, Ronald Reagan would take his place at The Zane Grey Theatre. We never had the slightest doubt about what Gabby knew and when.

A few years later we bought a Motorola. By then I was trying to figure out why Mrs. Cleaver always wore pearls and high heeled shoes when she did her housework, and what exactly Wally and Eddie Haskill had in common besides homeroom and Butch Wax.

I didn't know it at the time but something important was happening to my imagination. Like The Incredible Shrinking Man, it was growing progressively smaller. Television did not require real attention. It was not something you did, it was something you had done to you. Other than a few random musings about the Cleavers, and the possible phylogenetic category of Topo Gigio, the act of watching television demanded no real exercise of the imagination. Television provided the words, but it also gave us the pictures.

When my parents were children they had not yet abandoned the radio. Families crowded into dimly lit parlors and listened to the sound of a creaking door that opened The Inner Sanctum. It was like storytelling among primitive tribesmen. When small children were asked "who knows what evil lurks in the minds of men," they conjured their own pictures. Who knows? The Shadow knows. And the images they fashioned from wants and fears were more lasting than the shadows I watched flickering across the Motorola a few decades later.

In the late '50s, my imagination was shrinking, but my naivete remained about standard size. I liked Ike, and we had not yet lost a war or a president. Black people had only recently been permitted to sit beside me on the number eight streetcar. Television in those years had provided the pictures, mostly of an America that never really existed. It was because of those pictures my imagination was no larger than the tiny screen on that first Admiral TV.

It was radio that made my imagination grow. At thirteen it provided me with a portable, Japanese way of escaping my parents. Motown and the Beatles provided the music. I provided the pictures. On hot summer evenings, I lay in bed and listened to Clint Courtney surround a foul pop or Willie Miranda go deep in the hole for a 6-4-3 double play. There was no need for instant replay because the pictures I manufactured were more magical and exciting than video tape would ever be. I still carry those pictures with me.

The late '60s and early '70s brought confusion, dissimulation and lots of unnecessary death. I returned to the tube to watch body counts every evening just before dinner. Presidents showed me their surgical scars or promised they were not crooks. By 1974 I was not sure I wished anyone else to provide the pictures again. With the exception of an occasional bug show on PBS, I was finished with television.

By my midtwenties I had reached the age when radio stations begin to be measured in terms of one's low threshold for musical pain. The hint of a single electric guitar imitating the amplified vocal cords of a tortured cat became the now longstanding sign that it is time to push the selection button.

Back then there was only one classical radio station in town. It was there I found Garrison Keillor, a man who looks like a high school chemistry teacher but is blessed with a voice made by God and given to him for the purpose of radio.

In his weekly broadcasts I began to have very clear ideas about the looks of Bertha's Kitty Boutique and the green sock hanging in front of Bob's Bank. Keillor provided the words; I still have the pictures. Listening to his program allowed one to remember just how important and powerful the art of storytelling can be. In a real way Keillor reinvented the radio tale. For the briefest of times, he reassembled the primitives around the campfire. I knew, of course, that the town of Lake Wobegon existed in that province of the imagination, that it only existed as long as Keillor was saying it. But its transitoriness made it all the more valuable.

Now, twice a month or so, I put together a little essay for the new classical radio station in Baltimore. I have discovered the differences between writing for the reader and writing for the listener are enormous. In reading, the words appear like little sign posts across the page. If you get lost, it is easy to double back to the beginning of a sentence to find your way. In radio, words are like vapors. They hang in the air for the briefest of moments until they dissipate. They must be memorable enough to be trapped instantly in the imagination, like flying insects imprisoned in blown glass. This difference makes writing for the radio like giving directions to someone waiting in the dark. Writing long, complicated sentences for the listener is like spinning around a blind-folded child at a birthday party and expecting him to find the back end of a donkey.

Another important difference between the radio and the printed page is the added dimension sound makes. On the page, all the characters look alike. They stand in rows as if at attention. If I write the word "Bang!" the reader must translate it into the sound. The sound is private because the translation occurs in the hollow of an individual head. It is not a public sound. In radio, the words themselves are sounds, and thus they are more immediate and something shared.

Radio does not provide shared pictures; it provides shared sounds, and it is the variety of the sounds, in addition to the spoken voice, that perhaps is the most striking difference. When I write a piece for the newspaper about chirping cicada, the words sit on the page like dogs on graduation day at the obedience school. There is no movement and no sound. But when I speak a piece over the radio about chirping cicada, the producer may have them chirping unobtrusively in the background. This possibility of using sounds and various voices does for the narrator of a tale what the invention of new primary colors might do for the landscape painter.

But these differences between my printed pieces and the radio essays should not obscure what is perhaps the most important similarity they share. In both media I try to tell good stories—tales about small events and those that often overwhelm the most thoughtful of us. My little broadcasts are an attempt at capturing large and small moments worth carrying around. They allow me to provide the words in a completely new way. It also permits me to add a few wonderful sounds. But it is still the listener who must provide the pictures.

*April, 1988*

# Odd Glitches

The world we live in, I've come to realize, is an exceedingly strange place, but I've been part of the strangeness for so long I tend to take it for granted. Every now and then, the immensely peculiar nature of the planet and those of us who walk around upright on it becomes crystal clear. I'm convinced that these experiences that remind us of the peculiar nature of things are very different from the profound tales of the great religious prophets. They don't really mean anything more than what they are: anomalies, odd glitches, gravy stains on the cosmic wallpaper. Consider these three experiences I've had in the past week.

Early in the week, I saw an old high school friend who now works as an advertising executive in a large New York firm. After dinner we returned to her grandmother's home where my friend was spending the night. I'd always considered the grandmother to be an urbane, genteel woman, the kind with immutable blue hair and stoic constitution. When we returned from dinner the old woman had waited up for us so she could do her imitation of the emperor of Japan. During the impersonation, which she performed in her bathrobe, the matron popped out her false teeth to get the proper effect. At the end of the performance, the old woman reinserted her teeth and said, "Ah, I suppose he can't help it."

A few moments later while in the bathroom, I discovered that the grandmother had, in fact, three different pairs of false teeth. The first jar atop the toilet tank was marked, BEST PAIR. It was empty. Presumably this is the set she uses for her Japanese impersonations. The other two jars contained disembodied sets of porcelain choppers. One jar was labeled NEXT BEST. The third was marked NOT BAD.

This is clearly one of those experiences one cannot make up. The following day another one happened. I went into a stationery store to buy some paper. In came a frail mouse-of-a-woman carrying a small pocket calendar. She waved it in front of the shopkeeper and proclaimed, "This calendar's missing November!" The shopkeeper was undaunted and pointed out to the mouse lady that she had bought the calendar in January and that thus she wasn't entitled to a refund. The mouse lady responded sadly, "When you buy a pocket calendar, you don't check to see if it has a November." The shopkeeper responded quite indignantly, "Well, I really don't see what the problem is. Besides Thanksgiving, nothing ever happens in November."

After these two incidents I thought I'd received my ration of cosmic accidents for the next decade or so. That was until the following evening.

At a very posh dinner party in Roland Park, I was seated next to a very dignified looking older man, who some time after the main course fell asleep and began to list in my direction. By the dessert, his head rested comfortably on my shoulder. As the man was a widower, he had no wife to rebuke him. The strange thing about the man was he was not only missing a wife, he was missing an arm. And one might have thought by the simple law of gravity, that he would lean in the direction of the arm, and thus into the lap or onto the shoulder of my hostess. In point of fact, he listed in the direction of the armless side. His head eventually propped on my shoulder. What makes this tale even more peculiar is that he nodded off in the midst of a story I was telling about an old lady with three pairs of false teeth and a woman who lost November.

*November, 1986*

# K-Mart and Neurosurgery

The other afternoon, during a break in one of my summer classes, a student casually mentioned she was to have some dental work done at Sears. At first I thought she was kidding. Students frequently tell their professors outrageous lies. It is part of what the folks in the admissions office call "the college experience." Many of these tales involve the mysterious and tragic death of a grandmother during final exams. I have taken to advising my students to keep their elderly relatives out of harm's way until after the end of the school year. I consider it a kind of public service announcement.

I can usually discern when my students are not telling the truth. They flash that same look on their faces my dog has when I ask him in my most incriminating voice whether he has thrownup on the porch. Since the young woman was without the tell-tale look, and since she was talking about having *her* teeth checked at Sears and not those of her grandmother, I was pretty sure she was being forthright with me.

With a little more conversation, I discovered that in addition to having her dental work done at Sears, she also had her eyes examined at Wards.

Now this is not the sort of opportunity a writer can easily pass up. Frequently, well-meaning friends and acquaintances walk up to me and say, "You know, you really *ought* to write about ____." In most cases, I don't know anything about ____. The reason I know nothing about ____ is that I have never found it even in the most remote way interesting. Whenever I do know a little about ____, I usually think what I do know about it is silly and certainly not worthy of the weighty obligation words like "ought" imply. Dental work at Sears and eye care at Wards seems like a much more appropriate topic than _____, so I decided I really *ought* to write an essay about it.

Upon still further investigation, however, I discovered that not only will Sears provide dental work and Ward optometry services—you can also get your hair done, rent a car, buy insurance, acquire investment advice, or hire a lawyer at one or the other of these places. I think Caldor and K-Mart are missing out on something really big here. Think of all those other medical specialties that are not yet taken. "Attention K-Mart shoppers, now during the blue-light special, in row nine, brain surgery." Or what about: "Welcome to Caldor, 40 to 60% off during our Washington's Birthday Sale on all procedures in our obstetrics and gynecology department."

If this idea caught on it could be really good for the economy. The physicians at K-Mart and Caldor could run over to Sears to get their malpractice insurance. They could drop off their old policies and while the guys in the Sears Insurance Department saw if they could do better than the traditional malpractice companies, the doctors could have their hair done, or get some investment advice.

In the meantime, the patients from Caldor and K-Mart could walk over to Wards to find a good lawyer. If they won their malpractice suits, the plaintiffs could take their money over to Sears for investment advice. Maybe the physicians could put the whole settlement on their Wards Credit Card. I wonder if Mr. Roebuck is sorry he didn't think of any of this.

*July, 1988*

# The Department of Lost Belongings

Sometimes the physical world reminds us of how little control we have over it by making things disappear. It is because of human pride we often say that *we* have lost these objects when, in reality, *they* really have vanished.

We have all had this experience: we misplace our keys or a favorite pen, a book, a pair of eyeglasses, or any other object of disappearing size. A moment later the item has vanished. We usually say these things have disappeared "into thin air." There is apparently something about thick air that normally keeps these objects from defying the regular laws of physics.

The item was on the table a moment ago. But that was when life had a sort of order to it. That was when the world had an impeccable structure with regard to things physical. But now the order has vanished—along with the keys, the pen or the eyeglasses.

After each of these strange disappearances—and they happen quite often to the objects in my life—I resort to methods of discovery my intellect tells me are crazy. I first search beneath the largest articles of furniture in the house. These are pieces too big for any single human being to move. Next I look carefully amid the cushions on my sofa. I have not sat on my sofa since 1972, but I decided at the time, like most Americans, I would never do any living in the living room. In fact, I'm planning on having my living room hermetically sealed, but that is another story. After I search frantically through the cushions, I usually look in the toilet, in the refrigerator and sometimes in the mailbox. These are not the acts of a rational man. They are more akin to the ritual behavior of primitive tribesmen. The logic is really quite simple: if an object disappears in some strange, irrational way, one must first look in strange and irrational places. Because it would make too much sense to find them there, we never do.

When I was a small Catholic school child, the next step in my search was always to look under my bed. After that I usually prayed to Saint Anthony. If the lost item was not under the bed, nor could it be restored by the patron saint of lost things, I figured the object had been permanently consigned to metaphysical oblivion.

In adulthood I have finally arrived at a tentative theory about where all my lost belongings might be. I think all the objects that have mysteriously disappeared over my life have gone to the same place. It looks much like a lost-and-found department, where the found part has been lost. I think each of us has his own bin. They are probably in alphabetical order.

My department is filled with shelves of books, student papers, parking tickets, important forms from the dean's office, various articles of clothing and money in all denominations. The compartments situated near mine—those of my brother and his wife, for example—are nearly empty. The little people in charge of their lost department mostly play cards all day and wonder how they lucked into such cushy jobs. The man responsible for my lost belongings, however, is concerned these days about running out of space. He has sent his boss a series of urgent memos, written on my stationery, about the possibility of building an annex to my lost bin.

If the little man is denied his request, he may have to return all my stuff. Imagine all those items reappearing at my house at the same time. Now that is a scary thought. All of these objects will probably re-materialize in my living room. It will more than likely happen after I have had the room hermetically sealed.

*December, 1988*

# Stretch Limousines

I have wondered lately just how far the concept of a stretch limousine can be stretched. A few years back, when these elongated limos first began to be sited, I mistakenly believed there were an inordinately large number of funerals passing through my neighborhood. But when I gradually came to realize the passengers in these vehicles were, for the most part, travelling upright and without their headlights on, I had to abandon my mortuarial theory.

Before the mid-seventies, with the exception of those people in the business of giving us our last ride, the average limousine was just a big black Cadillac and a guy with a funny hat at the wheel. Since then, the concept of a limousine has grown, so that the average limo now looks like your basic United States Navy aircraft carrier with optional tinted windows.

One thing that can be said for the stretch limousine phenomenon is that it has spawned a whole new growth industry, if you'll excuse the expression. Men have been put back to work building stretch garages. Cadillac dealerships all over America have employed people to construct extensions for their show rooms. Car wash employees and street people who clean windshields at stoplights have experienced some of the economic trickle down from the elongation of the American limousine. And surely, all of this is good for the economy.

But recently William F. Buckley, in an article for the *New Yorker,* revealed that he had sent his new stretch limo to a man in New Mexico who added another foot or so to the body of the car.

Mr. Buckley's action has stirred in me a great concern. In short it is this: just how far can the concept of a stretch limousine be stretched? Surely at some critical point the fully stretched limousine, some might say the overstretched limousine, must become the automotive equivalent of the dachshund—those tragic little dogs with too much in the middle and not enough at either end to make the whole thing go. Indeed, if the stretch limousine is already spread too thin, it poses a real and present danger to contemporary American culture. What happens if these elongated limos, due to the basic laws of physics, all begin to snap back to about the size of a Plymouth Valiant? Most of the major corporations in America would be without their movers and shakers—the remnants of martini glasses, Gucci loafers, mobile phones, and chief operating officers all pressed together in some horrible approximation of the limousines' back seats. This might be good for the funeral industry, but it clearly would not help the overall economy.

The danger of this sort of thing happening looms larger every day. There are now so many stretch limousines in the great eastern cities of the United States alone that if you put them end to end they would stretch around Mr. Buckley's ego twice, or around the entire world four times, whichever you prefer.

Actually, this stretching around the world might be a very good idea. It would be good for our foreign policy initiatives, as well as having a salutary effect on the international economy, particularly if other nations were smart enough to install parking meters along the route.

*March, 1988*

# The Return of Mundane Mysteries

In an essay published last year I revealed the existence of a file folder marked "Mysteries, mundane" that sits in my grey file cabinet between "Mysore" and "Mysticism." In the essay I revealed some of the content of the file and asked for assistance from anyone who has answers to questions like "What are the rules for who gets the armrests at the movies?" and "What are the buttons for on electrical poles at crosswalks?"

Rather than simply answering these questions, many people responded to my request by either reprimanding me for spending time on such silly and insignificant matters or, worse, they sent along more mundane mysteries. This last kind of response, of course, is a bit like dropping off some airless tires to a man stranded on the highway with two flats.

And so, in an effort to thin out my "M" drawer, not to mention helping some others who have sent along their own mysteries, I offer the following, plucked fresh from the file for your consideration.

(1) There is a sign by the side of the road, in Baltimore, on Hilton Parkway, traveling west, just before a long, sweeping curve. It reads: "Keep Car Under Control Next 1/4 Mile."

This is not like some signs brought to us by dropouts from sign painter's punctuation class, things like: "Slow Men Working" or "Slow Children at Play." No, this is a genuine mundane mystery. What could this sign possibly mean? What are we to do after the 1/4 mile?

(2) Why do divorce lawyers call themselves "family practice" attorneys? Doesn't this make about as much

sense as a condom company called "The Virginity Guarantee Corporation?"

(3) An automotive mystery: Why do Americans park in driveways and drive on parkways?

(4) Another automotive conundrum: Does anyone know what those announcers are actually saying in the last ten seconds of radio advertisements for automobiles? The first twenty seconds of these spots are done in a human voice at regular speed. The last ten seconds are supplied by Alvin the Chipmunk on Benzedrine: thisofferincludesno windshieldwiperstiresoranythingelseexceptafewminorenginepartsandtwoaxelsitisbasedonacontractat$5000downand $300amonthfor50yearsortherestofyourlifewhicheverislongest.

(5) What is the difference between flammable and inflammable?

(6) Who named that spot at the crook of one's elbow the funny bone? Why it is never funny when one hits oneself there? Are the funny bone and the crazy bone the same bone? Was the person crazy who named it the funny bone?

And finally: (7) Are there any human beings alive who know the words to the 1960s song "Louie, Louie" by the Kingsmen? When I was in college I went to lots of parties where I'd drink enormous quantities of beer and pour it over the heads of like-minded scholars. Toward the end of the evening, we'd stomp around the dance floor, all screaming, "Louie, Louie,...oh no...we gotta go...I yai yai yai..."

For several years after college I lived under the false belief that the reason I did not know all the words to the song had something to do with drinking all that beer and stomping around the dance floor for several hours, that under these circumstances it was a medical curiosity of sorts that I stayed conscious at all. But the other day, while driving home from school, the truth once again reared its ugly head. "Louie, Louie" came on the radio, and I began to sing along, only to find that I still couldn't understand anything other than the "we gotta go" part.

If there is someone out there who knows the words to this song, you may also be able to tell me if the proper spelling is "Louie, Louie" or "Lou-E, Lou-I." The Kingsmen seem to prefer the latter pronunciation.

Please don't send me more mundane mysteries. I hope to hear from you. In the meantime, I gotta go...I yai yai yai.

*August, 1987*

# The Real Mr. Potato Head

Last year about this time I wrote something about my search for Lincoln Logs. As a child I owned several sets and thought they might made a good present for a friend's son.

I went to the toy store with the dyslexic giraffe out front. After an hour of searching, I found the Lincoln Logs, but they were not quite what I remembered.

What made the trip even more disheartening was the realization that many of the toys I loved as a child were nowhere to be found. It took me just about a year to get over the loss of Mexican jumping beans and the little acrobat who did a flip when one pressed two sticks together joined by a skinny string. The passing of these toys was like the loss of childhood friends and it told me more than I wanted to know about contemporary American childhood.

And so it was with a bit of the Old Testament girding of the loins that I entered the Toys-backward-R-Us. It was only a moment later the bad news began: Mr. Potato Head no longer requires the use of a real potato. Clearly, this creates something of what the analytic philosophers call a problem of identity reference. How in good conscience can we continue to use the name Mr. Potato Head for a toy that comes with a lump of molded plastic to replace the part formerly played by a real honest-to-God potato? At the very least the box should be marked "Mr. Plastic Potato Head." Or, better still, it should come with program notes which state, "The part formerly played by a real potato is now played by a piece of ugly molded plastic."

As if the elimination of a real potato were not enough, the piece of molded plastic also comes with preselected holes where the obedient and unimaginative child is to place the eyes, ears, nose, mouth and little eye glasses, so as to construct the face of the ugly Mr. Plastic Potato Head. In my childhood one of the most wonderful things about Mr. Potato Head was that the child could place the eyes, ears, nose and mouth anywhere he or she liked, often creating potatoes like Salvador Dali might have made if he were God.

If one put enough holes in it, and if one managed to convince his mother to keep it around long enough, Mr. Potato Head would grow older. After a couple of weeks, he looked shriveled up and toothless, a sort of vegetable version of Gabby Hayes. Kept another week or so, the potato skin began to act as a metaphor for the way of all flesh.

But the most wonderful thing about the real Mr. Potato Head was its propensity to roll under the couch, where it would lie undisturbed for two or three months. By the time it was rediscovered, Mr. Potato Head mysteriously had grown hair. This fascinated the children at my house to no end but left my mother quite disgusted. If Mr. Plastic Potato Head rolled under the couch and we didn't discover him for another 2,000 years, he would look exactly the same except for a thick coating of dust.

A few minutes after coming to grips with the saga of the real Mr. Potato Head, I made a second unfortunate discovery: horse shoes are now made of plastic. Don't the makers of plastic horse shoes know that the most important thing about horse shoes is the sound they make? Imagine the sound of a plastic horse shoe ringing a plastic stake sticking out of a pit constructed of indoor-outdoor carpeting. This is not the sort of experience of which summer camp memories are made.

Over in another corner of the store I found something called a Hop Scotch Kit. I know you are thinking: "What could possibly come in a Hop Scotch Kit besides a piece of chalk stolen from school and a cat's paw heel borrowed from your father's dress shoes?" The answer is that a Hop Scotch Kit comes complete with a large plastic sheet, outlined with perfect boxes from one to ten, thus eliminating the need for the piece of chalk and any use of the child's imagination. The kit also includes a piece of ugly molded plastic to play the part of the cat's paw. No longer will "sevensees" look more like a rhombus than a square. The Hop Scotch Kit has taken care of that.

On my way out of the store I found an intergalactic replacement for Monopoly. No longer will we pretend to own pieces of Atlantic City, New Jersey, before there is anything there. The new game, which is subtitled, "The Space Age Game of Real Estate," provides our children with the possibility of becoming slum landlords of planets or even entire galaxies.

I left the store in a state of depression. It made me yearn for the real Mr. Potato Head. It made me want to crawl under the couch for a few months and grow some hair.

*December, 1988*

# Alphabetical Discrimination

Recently, while standing in line for an academic procession—that strange parade of unwilling and unlikely peacocks—a member of the music department, an energetic and omni-capable woman, asked me why I had never written anything about alphabetical discrimination. I knew immediately what she was talking about. Her last name begins with Z. For decades we both, as victims of rare recognition and frequent discrimination, have suffered through the misfortune of being born to families clustered at the wrong end of the alphabet.

My youth was spent in a collection of classrooms filled with alphabetized students. Those at the end of the parade of twenty-six letters almost always were shunted off to the cheap seats. Merit badges, Holy Communions, Confirmations, and graduations were all dispensed according to the well-worn practice that the last shall be last, and the Zs shall inherit the leftovers.

While the Bs and Cs received early and enthusiastic applause for having the good fortune to graduate early in the ceremony, the Vs and Zs languished in a kind of alphabetical limbo. By the time the academic ship had docked at the port of last call, the parents of the Fs and Gs were finishing the first course of the graduation dinner. Those parents in the early part of the alphabet who did not sit close enough to an exit usually lapsed into a state of semi-consciousness, narcolepsy reigning by the Hs.

Even now, otherwise sensitive, articulate, and socially conscious souls rarely understand the slights of those consigned to the back of the alphabet. Indeed, why is it called the alphabet? Remember, if you will, that *alpha* is the first letter of the Greek system. And why do we call the entire collection of English letters the ABCs? Why do they get special billing?

For those of you Gs and Fs who find all this amusing, just ask yourself how you would like to be perpetually at the end of everyone else's rolodex. It is not an accident that the last ten letters of the English alphabet do not appear in alphabet soup.

Woody Allen, in an attempt at making a sensitive end-run around the problem of top billing, listed the actors in his new film in alphabetical order. Can you guess whose name appears first on the list? I wonder if he would have employed this supposedly egalitarian solution if his name were Allen Woody.

Jesus, a sensitive man, but a C nevertheless, suggests that at the end of time the first shall be last and the last first. If he is right, Aaron Aaronson is in for a big surprise. I hope he brings some magazines.

*December, 1989*

# On Seeing Time

> *The gods confound the man who first found out how to distinguish hours. Confound him too who in this place sets up a sun dial to cut and hack my days so wretchedly into small portions.*
> —Plautus (200 B.C.)

In a few moments it will be 1990, the beginning of a decade ushered in, while in the same instant the '80s are given the bum's rush. *Homo sapiens,* we time-keeping creatures, are fond of collecting time in increments, storing it up in decades and centuries, but we have not always been such *kronos* collectors.

The ancient Greeks, a people who had two words for time, saw it as a kind of cosmic odometer. Their time clicked away its temporal tenths of a mile until it all rolled back to zero, starting the entire process over again in a kind of eternal return.

In ancient India, the matter was not much different. The beginning and the end of an eon were billions of years apart and yet mysteriously tied back together like a dim-witted dog chasing its tail.

It is Augustine, the fifth-century Christian philosopher whom many credit with our Western linear conception of time, a time measured in discreet, definable segments never to be repeated. Since Augustine's time, events march forward in the West, the past receding over the last hill never to be seen again. Francis Bacon in his essay, "Of Innovation," suggests that Augustine's discovery of linear time was simultaneously a founding of the very landscape of experience. Only by marking off segments of a life does its meaning come into clear focus. But Augustine did not take credit for inventing time; he suggested it was one of God's good ideas.

Perhaps this is why the fifth-century bishop of Hippo assumed such a reverent attitude toward time. He held it in awe, as elusive and mysterious as a cat's thoughts. "What, then, is time?" Augustine asks in Book XI of his *Confessions,* "If no one asks me, I know. If I want to explain it to a questioner, however, I do not know what it is."

The elusiveness of time, in a way, is not so different from another great mystery—the paradox of motion. In theory we are all aware that the earth revolves. But in practice we do not perceive it. The ground upon which we tread seems not to move, and thus we live undisturbed. So it is with time. We move through our everyday lives and it passes steadily, secretly, unless, like this evening, we have cause to pay it some notice. Time beats for all, to paraphrase John Donne, and yet we seem only to reflect upon it when it becomes palpable.

The most obvious way time becomes real is in watching the sweep of a second hand. In the movement we *see* time. In this sense, the wearers of digital watches are cheated out of an important way in which time is made real. The digital time piece dooms the wearer to apprehending static instants. What is lost is the forward motion provided by the silent sweep of the second hand

But there are other ways in which time can unmistakably be seen. Think of apprehending a dear friend after several years absence. In an instant we see something the friend must have stared at for years every morning in the bathroom mirror, and yet, did not really see. If time is, as Tennyson insists, a maniac scattering dust, then the madman makes his deposits a few grains at a time. It is only the cumulative effect to which we pay any real notice.

Lately (a wonderfully ambiguous expression to which analytic philosophers have given the weighty name "a temporal indexical"), I have come to understand that, if we will look, we have the opportunity to see time in a variety of ways. The Sunday *New York Times* sits on my desk. It occupies a space just next to a copy of Plato's *Apology*. The edition of the *Times* is about 4,000 pages, 200,000 words in all. The *Apology* is a very light 2,340 words, and yet, there is something in the juxtaposition of the two where time becomes palpable. The newspaper, later this evening, or perhaps in the morning, will be transformed into heat in the fireplace. The newspaper, except in the hands of coupon clippers and new brides, rarely lasts beyond the day. The *Apology*, I should hope, will be here long after the concept of a newspaper has taken its place alongside cuneiform tablets as an interesting anachronism.

Imagine an enormous rock formation somewhere in Montana—a flat surface that juts out into an overhang. Beneath the formation, protected by the ancient overhang, a solitary camper has pitched his pale blue tent for the evening. In the morning, the tent will be gone. In the morning, the rock will remain, dumb, inert, but eternal.

There is, in all of us, a desire to be the rock, invulnerable, timeless, but aware. We wish to project ourselves out into time, an eerie time precisely because it will not really contain us. As I sit here at my desk, I think of New Year's Day 2050. By then, I, and most of my acquaintances and those I love, will be done in by the madman's dust. I run ahead in time to see what Stephen Vicchio as a memory might be like. I try it for a few moments and then gravity or grief seems to short-out my temporal circuits.

These kinds of exercises in seeing time have begun to occupy an ever larger part of my consciousness. Perhaps it comes with the thought that in this year, that strange 365-day journey around the sun, I will be forty. In this year I will keep a close watch on the heavens, I will keep track of the changing faces of the stars so that I might better *see* time.

*December, 1989*